The Electric Guitar Handbook

Rod Fogg

A BACKBEAT BOOK
First edition 2009
Published by Backbeat Books
An Imprint of Hal Leonard Corporation
7777 West Bluemound Road,
Milwaukee, WI 53213
www.backbeatbooks.com

Devised and produced for Backbeat Books by
Outline Press Ltd
2A Union Court, 20-22 Union Road,
London SW4 6JP, England
www.jawbonepress.com

ISBN: 978-0-87930-989-3

A catalogue record for this book is available from the British Library.

DESIGN: Paul Cooper Design
EDITOR: John Morrish

Origination and print by Regent Publishing Services Limited, China

09 10 11 12 13 5 4 3 2 1

contents

■ introduction

I'd like to welcome you to *The Electric Guitar Handbook*: a systematic, progressive, and all-encompassing approach to learning the guitar. The tutorial assumes no prior musical knowledge; it begins at the very beginning with lessons that will be playable by students with no musical experience whatsoever. Lessons are taught using real music rather than tedious or un-musical technical exercises, and you can listen to the musical examples on the accompanying CD. If you have already begun learning the guitar you can make faster progress through the earlier parts of the book before finding your level. If you are completely new to guitar playing, you can progress at your own speed, taking on as much or as little work as you can manage. If you come to something difficult, you can keep going forwards while returning regularly to earlier pieces that you found challenging.

All the musical examples in this book are presented in both standard musical notation and guitar tablature. Both of these parallel forms of notation receive a thorough explanation, especially standard musical notation, which is so often glossed over in guitar tutorial books of this kind. Rather than commencing the book with endless pages of technical explanation and jargon, enough explanation is given at the beginning to get you started, and new matters are introduced and illustrated by musical examples as we progress through each section. In this way, progress is made simultaneously in three essential areas: technically on the instrument, theoretically in the understanding of music, and in the development of listening skills.

In the interests of making this book approachable to everyone, Part One begins with simple pieces of music involving initially only the open strings of the guitar, before adding single notes on the frets and learning to coordinate with the picking hand. Many other books begin with chords, but as chords involve the use of several left-hand fingers at once, they can be too challenging for the beginner. Chords are introduced in Part Two, including the interesting sounds that are available to the modern guitar player by extending and adding notes to standard chords. Strumming and picking are also examined in detail.

In Part Three, we return to single-note playing, but this time using the advanced techniques often found when playing riffs and soloing. Part Three also includes more advanced rhythm parts, including movable chord shapes that can be played all over the neck of the guitar. These are studied alongside the lead guitar parts so that we often have a playable two-guitar arrangement. Part Four combines all of the techniques learnt so far in a series of demonstrations of different styles of guitar playing, including blues, rock, metal, indie, funk, and so on.

I hope you will enjoy the music in this book and on the CD, and will have fun making steady progress in your guitar playing. I also hope you will take advantage of the opportunity to learn to read music. Although there are many guitarists in the rock world who claim not to be able to read music, it really is not that difficult, and it is a skill that you will never regret acquiring. There is nothing wrong with tablature; in fact tablature and notation work extremely well together. But the ability to read music will broaden your horizons and enable you to take on music from worlds as diverse as classical and jazz, as well as allowing you to read music that was not originally written for guitar.

Enjoy your journey.

Rod Fogg, *London 2008*

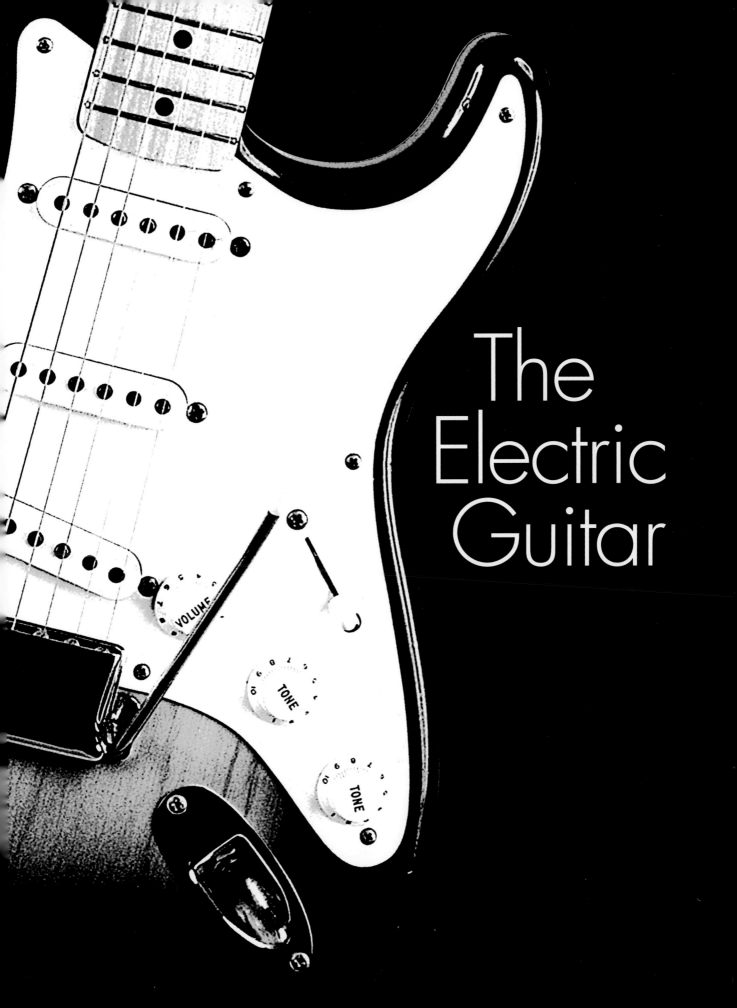

The Electric Guitar

the story of the electric guitar

THE ELECTRIFIED ARCH-TOP

The story of the electric guitar really begins with the electrified arch-top. Some makers had experimented with Hawaiian-style (lap steel) and standard solid and semi-solid electric designs even before arch-tops started receiving pickups at the factory, but those early adventures weren't the ones that carried amplification to the masses. Seemingly anathema today to anything pertaining to heavy music, the arch-top electric gave birth to rock'n'roll. Even before Fender's 'canoe paddle' and Gibson's 'plank' were invented, the acoustic-electric was bringing jazz, blues, and country swing guitarists out of the shadows – and before the fledgling solidbodies were fully accepted, it was still on hand to usher in a whole new way of playing.

Ernie Magann of The Paradise Islanders can be seen standing on the left playing his Rickenbacker Electro Silver Hawaiian steel guitar (above).

Three examples of early electrified arch-top guitars. A Gibson ES-150 from 1939 is on the right. In the center is a Rickenbacker Spanish (SP) from 1948. The full bodied Gibson ES-300 (far right) was made in 1941; this instrument was fitted with an unusual long pickup mounted on the body of the guitar at an acute angle.

Occasionally rather muddy of tone, lacking in sustain, and prone to howls of feedback, the 'electric Spanish' guitar, as it was generally first known, was nevertheless nothing short of a miracle in its day, and built the bridge to modern guitar music as we now know it. In the hands of a player like Charlie Christian – known for taking up Gibson's first electric model, the ES-150, almost from its arrival in 1936 – it gave the guitarist a means of competing with the horn player as a soloist … and finally being heard doing so. We have never looked back.

The first electrified arch-top models were essentially standard acoustic arch-tops with slightly adapted lap steel pickups bolted on to them. They retained the full-sized body and elaborate hand-carved spruce top, even though when amplified at the back of an orchestra in a large, crowded dancehall the tonal subtleties of the luthier's art weren't likely to be appreciated. Early production electrics from big makers like Gibson and Epiphone were still fully hand-built, but were generally somewhat low-end models compared to their upscale arch-top acoustic brethren. The makers saw no particular problem with this right from the start, because they still saw the electric guitarist as a fringe market, and even something of a novelty.

Two pages from Gibson's 1937 catalogue (above) feature the new ES-150 guitar with its associated amplifier and pictures of performers from the period showcasing Gibson products.

Amplified arch-top guitars came in many forms. The Gibson Super 400 acoustic from 1934 (far left) has a floating twin McCarty pickup that was added to the guitar in the 50s. The Gretsch Synchromatic model 6031 Tenor guitar was made in 1954 (center). The Gibson Super 400 CN-Wal dates from 1969 (left) and is fitted with a floating pickup that is not attached to the guitars body. There is still a demand for instruments of this type amongst jazz players today.

Even top-of-the-line electric models like Gibson's ES-300 or Epiphone's Zephyr lacked such niceties as the bound f-holes, deluxe trim, and upgraded hardware found on the acoustic-only L-5 and Emperor that were their respective contemporaries. Of course, as players of these and other high-end models decided they wanted to be heard too, Gibson Super 400s, Gretsch Syncromatics, and even D'Angelicos soon appeared with retro-fit pickups mounted to them. (At first these were generally of the less intrusive, 'floating' neck- or pickguard-mounted variety, still preferred by many traditional jazz guitarists today.)

The burgeoning awareness that the electric guitar was indeed a breed apart, with different requirements and capabilities, led naturally to the notion that acoustic-electrics could be designed to accentuate their electric qualities – while making

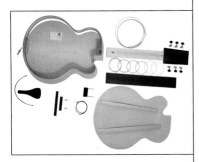

The differences in body construction between an electrified hollow-bodied guitar (top) and a solid-bodied electric guitar (below) can be clearly seen.

welcome cost savings through compromises in the acoustic department. Why go to the trouble and expense of hand-carving a spruce or maple top when you couldn't tell it from plywood after the body-mounted magnetic pickup and tube amp had dealt with the tone? In 1949 Gibson introduced its first electric with a pressed, laminated top in the form of the ES-175, which has since proved good enough for the likes of Joe Pass, Jim Hall, Pat Metheny, and many others.

Of course, the cheaper production techniques were not widely publicized at the time. But as well as providing savings at the factory, the use of laminated woods gave the guitars a brighter, snappier edge than their predecessors, which suited amplification even better for many purposes. A number of rival manufacturers followed suit with laminated construction and it quickly became the standard for acoustic-electric arch-tops.

Still thought of first and foremost as a jazz box, and a rare breed in the rock arena – despite the efforts of noisemongers like Ted Nugent and Billy Duffy, or prog-rock whiz Steve Howe – it behoves us to remember what a revolution-in-the-making the acoustic-electric was half a century ago or more in the hands of Scotty Moore, Chuck Berry, or T-Bone Walker.

THE SOLIDBODY ELECTRIC

It's difficult to conceive of rock without the solidbody electric guitar, even though the instrument was developed before that radical musical genre even existed, and initially aimed at another breed of player entirely. Although rock'n'roll was born on big-bodied arch-tops with pickups mounted on top, the limitations of these instruments were clear. For real power with volume and attack, enough brightness to cut through the clutter, and a sound free from the severe restraints of feedback, solidbodies proved the only way forward.

They were scorned, jeered at, derided and generally shown little respect by the traditional guitar-playing masses of the day. But the introduction of early solidbody designs in the 30s and 40s and the arrival of the first mass-produced solidbody electric guitar in 1950, the Fender Broadcaster, nevertheless represented a revolution in the making. The sound, the look, and the sheer volume of popular music would never be the same again.

Two examples of the solid-bodied electric guitar: an early Fender Telecaster from 1953 (left) and a 1976 Telecaster Deluxe (right), a later variant of this classic instrument fitted with twin humbucking pickups.

The strong graphic feel of the cover of Fender's 1955 catalogue shows the outline of the Telecaster guitar and evokes the period (top right).

FENDER BROADCASTER AND TELECASTER

As with all of his early successes in the manufacture of electric instruments and amplification, Leo Fender arrived at the first mass-production solidbody guitar by a combination of careful R&D, clever artist liaison, and happy accident. A mere stylized rendering of the existing guitar, the Broadcaster (which by mid-1951 and forever after was known as the Telecaster) took the concept of the instrument back to the drawing board, preserving little more than its six strings, scale length, and standardized tuning.

The essentially acoustic 'electrics' by Gibson, Epiphone, Gretsch, and others were great instruments but had inherent limitations that were still making it difficult for guitarists to step front-of-stage and seriously compete as soloists. The relatively dark, often muddy sound of these guitars could get lost amid the brass sections of large

The original version of this mass-produced solid-bodied electric guitar from Fender. This early version, named the Broadcaster, was made in 1950 (above).

The unique aspect of Leo Fender's design was the bolt-on neck, which allowed easy replacement and fine adjustment to be made on the road. The original four-bolt joint that attached the neck to the guitar's body can be seen from the back (above). Fender changed briefly to a three-bolt neck joint in 1968 (above right).

In 1954, Fender produced the Stratocaster, a solid-bodied electric guitar with three pickups, mainly in response to public demand for more sonic versatility. The instrument utilized the four-bolt neck/body joint that can be seen in the rear view (center). Also visible is the 'body fitting' sculptured rear, which can be compared with that of the 'slab-sided' Telecaster body (far right).

western swing orchestras and smaller jazz combos alike, and they were prone to howls of feedback when turned up loud enough to be heard in larger halls.

Leo Fender's Telecaster had improved pickups, a treble-enhancing, sustain-encouraging, and highly adjustable bridge design, and resonant through-body stringing in a solid ash body. It combated all the limitations of the acoustic-electric and gave guitarists the chance to be heard on a grand scale. (Similar models followed from most of Fender's major competitors.) Furthermore, the rugged construction and the screw-off, screw-on repairability of nearly every part on the Telecaster made it a workhorse able to withstand the knocks of the road and be easily serviced when the need arose. Coupled with that, the instrument's slim, fast neck and easy action introduced exciting new levels of playability.

Originally devised to save labor and make repair or replacement simpler, the 'bolt-on-neck' guitar (the neck is in fact screwed on) has a tonality all its own. It offers a bright, edgy, cutting tone (the classic 'twang'), a woody resonance, and decent natural sustain (particularly from through-body designs), as well as good tuning stability. A total success in design terms, this early model has remained popular both in its original and modified forms for 60 years now, and has established the bolt-neck guitar – in all its variations – as one of a number of tonal standards, and not just a maintenance convenience.

Not only did the new era in guitar construction help make the guitar the star in dozens of popular country and swing bands, it saw the electric guitar virtually taking the job of an entire orchestra, ushering in guitar groups (typically two guitars, a bass, and drums) that would change the face of popular music forever and pave the way for rock'n'roll. More than merely a point of evolution in the look and feel of the instrument, the solidbody electric triggered a giant leap in the sound and power of the guitar-based band. There was little point developing large, high-powered amplifiers when guitars would only squeal with feedback after a certain volume was reached. With the solidbody, suddenly the sky was the limit in amp design – and in the volume wars the guitar was the new victor.

Since those early days, countless other brands have followed the form of Fender's production-line original, and it has proved – with a number of variations – to be one of the most successful templates for the solidbody electric guitar.

FENDER STRATOCASTER

Gibson's Les Paul managed to do most everything that Fender's Telecaster could do, if somewhat differently (see below). So Fender needed a new trick to bring the spotlight back in their direction. In 1954, with the launch of the Stratocaster, they found it. While the Tele set the prototype for bolt-neck solidbody electrics, the Strat took the format right out of this world, introducing the most-played and most-copied electric guitar design of all time.

Aside from its radical shape, if the Strat had been fitted with Tele pickups and hardware it would have sounded and performed much like a Tele. But two major areas of design development – in electronics and hardware – significantly altered the instrument's sound and playability.

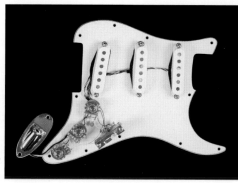

Three bright-sounding pickups and three-pickup switching are combined with a very efficient adjustable vibrato (far left). The pick-ups, wiring loom, and switching are shown removed from the body (left).

A fine original example of a 1957 Fender Stratocaster showing the standard sunburst finish (below).

The first innovation came in the Strat's electronics. New pickups, ostensibly much like the single-coil units on the Telecaster, were developed by Fender for the Stratocaster. They were brighter, with sharper highs (though often somewhat less powerful than the Tele bridge unit) in an era when cutting through a muddy bandstand 'mix' in order to be heard was a key priority. Also, the three-pickup switching with dual tone controls offered a broad range of voices.

Second, there was an even more radical advance: the Strat's fully-adjustable self-contained 'tremolo' tailpiece. This allowed more down-bend than any previously available production unit, in an age when heavier string gauges made left-hand bends more difficult, and offered good tuning stability when set up correctly. Even when not in use it changed the guitar's core tonality, shifting the path of string routing and tapping off some of the acoustic resonance through a bridge block and the unit's associated springs.

The Strat vibrato – now taken for granted – ushered in a whole new range of playing styles, from the new hard-twang country styles, through the heavily vibratoed surf instrumentals of the early 1960s, to Hendrix's wild divebombing and air-raid effects. Taken to new levels in subsequent decades by the likes of Eddie Van Halen and Jeff Beck, it has proved one of rock's most expressive tools.

In purely visual terms, the Stratocaster has become a design icon, honored and loved even by non-guitar players, and has a surprisingly timeless appeal. More than just a radical stylistic coup, however, the Strat's body contouring made it a more comfortable, even intimate, instrument to play. The upper back contour made it easier to tuck in under the ribcage for long sets, while the chamfer at the top of the lower bout braced the player's right forearm without cutting into it as a Les Paul or Tele's square edges did.

As familiar as we are today with the Strat's look, sound, and feel, any consideration of the inherent 'rightness' of all its ingredients reminds us once again of what a great leap forward Leo Fender's second solidbody represented at the time.

The Fender Stratocaster evolved into many variants over the last 50 years. Some of these versions are illustrated here in three Fender catalogues from the 80s (above).

The Strat has been the subject of countless upgrades and modifications, most of which have evolved into production models available off-the-shelf, including single and dual-humbucker models, locking nut and vibrato, deluxe wiring and switching layouts, and other 'superstrat' configurations. It remains the most emulated basic template for the solidbody electric more than 50 years after its arrival – and, in most cases, without straying radically from its original form.

GIBSON LES PAUL

Strap on a Les Paul today and one thing comes instantly to mind – and fingers: rock. It's incredible to think, then, that when the model arrived in 1952 there was no such music. Gibson's premier solidbody was a response to the growing success of the Telecaster. But, mindful of its reputation and eager to tap a market with more traditional players still put off by Fender's bolt-together radicalism, Gibson wasn't about to offer its own slab-styled canoe paddle.

Instead, Gibson applied its skill with carved arch-top 'jazz' guitars to a maple cap atop a solid mahogany body, sticking with its time-tested set neck construction, and attaching a pair of the P-90 pickups already in use on hollowbody f-hole models in the

Between 1958 and 1960 Gibson made around 1,600 of its Les Paul Standard Model with a maple top and a striking sunburst finish. This guitar has been reissued in many forms over the last 50 years. An early model from 1958 is shown here in near mint condition (facing page below).

The Gibson Les Paul started life as the solid-bodied Gold Top model in 1952. The earliest versions of the guitar were fitted with a crude trapeze tailpiece (far left). In 1957 the Gold Top was fitted with humbucking pickups, an adjustable bridge, and a stop tailpiece, making it a much more versatile instrument; a left-handed version is shown (center). The Les Paul is another classic instrument that has gone though numerous changes and variants. The Les Paul Voodoo model (left) is from 2004.

late 40s. In this way, Gibson arrived at the 'other electric' – the archetype for the solidbody with glued-in neck – and although they 'got it wrong' at first, with a flat neck angle and an awkward bridge that would soon be changed, the '52 Goldtop nevertheless established a new classic. Perceived as more elegant, with a big nod toward tradition but with all the power needed to pump out the new music, the Les Paul has evolved in many directions, but remains the third significant electric-guitar blueprint.

Several elements define the Les Paul's character, perhaps most important of which is its body construction. The chunky mahogany slab lends sustain and a generally warm, rounded resonance to the tone, given a degree of brightness and 'cut' by the carved maple top. Tonally, the glued-in neck aids sustain and sonic depth, and can introduce a certain darkness to the overall sound. As for playability, Gibson's neck pitch, or angle to the body, which is significantly steeper than that of Fender's, brings the neck more within reach of the left hand, which some players find more comfortable. The slightly shorter 24 ¾-inch (629mm) scale, meanwhile, also makes it somewhat slinkier and more bend-friendly than Fender's 25 ½-inch (648mm) scale length. However, the glued-in neck construction makes repairs and major adjustments difficult and often costly.

As for electronics, a Les Paul fitted with P-90 pickups is biting and edgy, with gritty highs and punchy mids. With humbuckers, it's generally a smooth, warm, powerful and sustaining guitar. Either way, output is hotter than standard Fender-type single-coil pickups, driving tube amps into distortion more quickly.

The Gibson-style solidbodies that followed the Les Paul, such as the Les Paul Special and Junior, Flying V, Explorer, and SG, along with roughly similar designs from other makers, leaned more toward slab body construction, and were cut from a single type of wood without the Les Paul's elaborate carved maple top. While the voice of some of these guitars is determined by body and neck woods, the set-neck joint which they share with the Les Paul still lends them a round, warm and full-throated tonality, particularly when partnered with humbuckers.

Manufacturers continue to produce guitars with fixed or 'set' necks that are glued into the body. The 1965 Gibson Les Paul Junior (left), the 1995 PRS Artist III (center), and the 1958 Gretsch Jet Firebird (right) all share this method of construction.

Stratocaster-style instruments featuring 24-fret necks, angular styling, locking vibrato systems, and modified pickup layouts are widely referred to as 'superstrats.' They are made by several different manufactures. Ibanez makes a range of this type of instrument, including the Steve Vai 777 Model featured in this catalogue page (right).

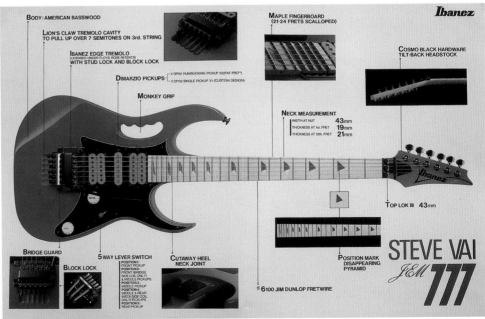

Guitar makers bring different design features to the standard bolt-on-neck instrument. Music Man added custom paint finishes, offset headstocks, and a mixture of single and double coil pickups with this Silhouette model from 1988 (left). Unusual materials, such as a chrome-finished synthetic 'luthite,' can be seen on the Ibanez JS 10th Anniversary (center). Simple classic design was used for the commercially successful Yamaha Pacifica range of guitars; this 604 Model dates from 1994 (near left).

Today, myriad combinations of bolt-on and set-neck designs provide tonal performance and playability that range between the two camps. Paul Reed Smith, for one, offers mahogany-bodied, carved-maple-topped designs with bolt-on necks; big rock-axe companies like Jackson and Ibanez build superstrat-style models with set-necks, hot humbuckers, and double-locking vibratos. With the borders demolished, it's no longer simply a matter of choosing between Fender and Gibson, although plenty of players continue to do exactly that.

THROUGH-NECK GUITARS

According to the prophecies of makers such as Ibanez, Yamaha, Alembic, Carvin, and a number of others in the late 70s and early 80s, the through-neck guitar was destined to be the 'way of the future'. They preached about added constructional stability, increased resonance and sustain, and an all-round improved instrument. The through-neck guitar was being touted as the new top of the line, the crème de la crème, the ultimate evolution of the solidbody electric guitar.

So what happened? Not a lot. Just as through-neck designs existed well before the 70s, they continue to be built today, but they've always been at the fringe of constructional techniques. Three things seem to account for this. First, the manufacturing complexities required of some designs didn't justify any 'improvements' gained over set-neck guitars – improvements that are, arguably, negligible anyway. Second, according to some builders and players, the apparent advantage of a central body core and neck carved from the same piece (or laminated pieces) of wood only proved detrimental to tone. And third? Well, these old bolt-on and set-neck guitars that were lying around all sounded pretty good already. Why go to the trouble of redesigning the wheel?

Used as a marketing tool around 1978, a 'through-neck' promised the ultimate in tone and sustain. In reality, many players noticed no quantifiable improvement in resonance, power, or general sound over glued-in or even bolt-on necks. Interestingly, many classic makes and models of solid or semi-acoustic electrics that employed through-neck construction in the late 50s and early 60s, notably a number of Rickenbackers and Gibson's first 'reverse body' Firebirds, usually did so without calling nearly as much attention to the fact.

Through-neck guitars have been made by many manufacturers including Gretsch; a version is pictured on the cover of its 1978 catalogue (top). Gibson used this construction method with its Firebird range of guitars (above). The best known through-neck builder is Alembic; the series I Model from 1978 is shown (right). Ibanez also made several guitars in this style; the Musician MC500 model was introduced in 1978 (far right).

There's little doubt, though, that the integral neck/body core design lends great structural stability to a well-built guitar, and the mere fact of the effort required to build a quality instrument using this technique generally signals that extra effort has been applied elsewhere, too. The strength of such a neck also makes it easier to design a guitar with deep cutaways and excellent upper-fret accessibility, since it's no longer necessary to leave enough solid body wood free from the upper and lower cutaway to secure a sturdy neck joint.

In any case, the major through-neck designs offered from the 70s onward tended to be high-end models, and generally powerful, weighty, humbucker-loaded guitars aimed at the rock or fusion player. Yamaha's SG-2000, first introduced in 1976, was the first Japanese guitar to gain wide acceptance among Western pros, with an important early endorsement from Carlos Santana. Even before this, Alembic – best known for deluxe active-electronics

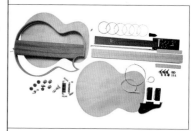

basses – was building some of the most expensive production solidbodies then available, all with through-neck designs, exotic woods, and elaborate active electronics. These designs further inspired more affordable models from Ibanez, Carvin, and others ... until the way forward was found by looking backward to 'retro' fashions, which have largely dominated electric guitar design over the last two decades.

SEMI-ACOUSTICS

Analyzed from the perspective of appearance and construction, the semi-acoustic would seem to represent an evolutionary step between the hollowbody arch-top electric and the solidbody electric that arrived in mass-produced form with the Fender Broadcaster of 1950. In form, at least, the 'semi' defines a step between the two: a hollowbody guitar, usually with an arched top, to which some wood has been added to enhance stability, sustain and feedback resistance. Taken chronologically, however, you could argue that the semi-acoustic is a solidbody from which some wood has been taken away. In theory, it is both of these. Other than a few one-offs, experiments, and prototypes (of which Les Paul's famous 'log guitar' was one), all of the more timeless semis arrived after Fender's groundbreaking, bolt-neck solidbody revolutionized the scene.

As used today, the designation 'semi-acoustic' relates to an instrument that usually employs the same or similar frontal dimensions as those of a full-size acoustic-electric – although proportions may be more compact – but with significantly slimmer body depth. The amount of air within can vary considerably; some guitars described as 'semis' (incorrectly, technically speaking) are completely hollow and are more correctly designated 'thinline hollowbodies', while others incorporate differing quantities of internal timber, ranging from small reinforcing blocks to full-length or full-width solid sections.

Those electrics that contain an appreciable amount of wood rather than open space may also be described as 'semi-solid,' which is where the duplication of terminology arises. On a strictly solid guitar, the body mass has a major effect on tonal properties and sustain, while the inherent natural sound of a full-depth acoustic-electric exerts a great influence on the character of its amplified output.

In keeping with its name, the semi (whether considered acoustic or solid) represents something of a halfway house between the two. The idea is that the resonance created in the hollow chambers of the body audibly contributes to the overall amplified performance. Even playing a semi 'unplugged' should reveal a louder acoustic response than that derived from a solid six-string, although it's still appreciably less than the volume produced by a deep-bodied, all-hollow equivalent. But this will of course only be of minimal importance when it comes to practical performance, because an amplifier will naturally negate any such discrepancies in volume.

Warranting much greater consideration are the overtones generated, because these can have a discernible effect on the end results – although it must

Guitars of a semi-acoustic construction sometimes have a separate solid block of wood running down the center of the body. It can be clearly seen in the component picture (above).

The Rickenbacker 381V69 from 1990 (below) has a thick carved top and internal acoustic chambers cut into the solid body from the back.

Semi-acoustic guitars were also referred to as 'thinlines,' and many examples were built without the solid central block. They include the Gibson Byrdland (right) from 1957, shown in the catalogue (above); the Gibson ES-225TDN, made in 1956 (center); and the 1959 Gibson ES-330 (far right).

be said that the differences so derived are more marked with some guitars than others. The aim is that these qualities should enhance rather than impede the sound, but exactly how such benefits are perceived and employed is really down to the individual player. In general, the semi-acoustic's extra resonance imparts a degree of sweetness and often mellowness to the sound, but with the low end staying well defined and treble content relatively unimpaired.

In recent years the semi-solid concept has become considerably more popular, with most company catalogues now offering at least one obviously more airy alternative. But to most players, the word 'semi' conjures up images of big but slim electrics, epitomised by the creations bearing the Gibson brand name. This company was the first to offer the convenience of thinner-bodied arch-top electrics, beginning with the Byrdland in 1955. The absence of much body depth made the instrument much more manageable, while still retaining the friendly familiarity of conventional cosmetics, and this policy was soon extended to include slender equivalents of existing instruments, including the ES-350T ('T' for 'thinline'), while the ES-225T was an even slimmer six-string. All employed single-cutaway styling, but in its size the 225 model paved the way for an innovative design approach.

In 1958 the company debuted the ES-335TD, featuring a body with novel twin cutaways and an internal solid centre block. Gibson correctly reasoned that the latter restricted the body's resonant properties, in turn reducing unwanted feedback, while also improving sustain. The end result was certainly less prone to the horrible howl, and while it was still not as safe as a full solidbody, it was at least a significant improvement, and also offered some of the sharper attack and longer sustain that solidbodies were becoming popular for. Almost at once Gibson exploited this advantage, adding the more deluxe ES-355TD and ES-345TD to make up a line of slimline semi-acoustics.

Also introduced at this time was the similarly styled but fully hollow ES-330TD, while sister brand Epiphone boasted respective equivalents in the form of the Riviera, Sheraton, and Casino. The popularity enjoyed by Gibson's twin-cutaway quartet soon prompted most competitors to revise their ranges. The slimline treatment had already been adopted by a great many makers worldwide, and the company would now exert even greater influence on styling.

Gretsch, Guild, and Harmony were among the many US manufacturers who opted to champion the twin-cutaway cause to a greater or lesser degree, usually adding their

Gibson and Harmony catalogues (above) promote their ranges of thinline semi-acoustic models.

Epiphone built semi-acoustics without central blocks, including the Sheraton E212TN from 1962 (far left) and the Supernova, made in 1997 (center). Gibson produced a range of popular semi-acoustics but added solid center blocks to most of them, including this early ES-335, which dates from 1959.

the electric guitar handbook

Variations on the semi-acoustic design came from a range of manufacturers. The Kay Jazz II was made in 1962 and featured in the catalogue below. Harmony made this H77 Model in 1964 (above). Gretsch made their Viking model in 1967 (center) and Guild continues to produce its Starfire model (far right); shown here is the Mark IV reissue from 2000.

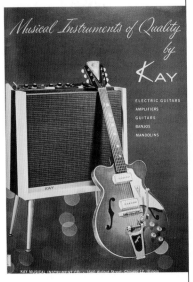

own touches to the overall outline. Surprisingly, none initially perceived the benefit of employing a solid centre block as Gibson did, although for a while Gretsch removed f-holes on some semis in an attempt to curtail feedback. Gibson's twin-cutaway concept was taken up by numerous contemporaries in many countries, with virtually all the European makers offering their own interpretations.

Again the constructional aspects were ignored in favor of retaining an all-hollow interior, but this position would change over the next two decades as the practical performance advantages became clear. The Japanese were quick to copy both cosmetics and construction methods for their more upmarket reproductions of the Gibson originals. The same principles were adopted when some of the makers in that part of the world decided to employ more original thinking, and the better examples of semis bearing brand names such as Aria, Ibanez, and Yamaha certainly put Gibson's groundbreaking work to good use.

More recently there has been a less slavish adherence to the long-established twin-cutaway styling, with Paul Reed Smith in particular breaking with tradition – at least visually – by applying new directions in semi-acoustic construction to its own familiar offset-cutaway body lines.

Regardless of price, most semi-acoustics employ laminated wood for the body front and back as this lends itself to the manufacturing methods involved. This contradicts the choice made for solids, where the use of plywood indicates penny-pinching production. Internal differences affect the choice of certain hardware components, and in many instances the bridge and tailpiece in particular can provide clues as to how much wood actually lurks within a semi. A floating bridge points to an all-hollow interior offering no purchase for body-mounted supports, and the same often applies to a trapeze-type tailpiece or vibrato unit secured to the end of the guitar.

Instruments that incorporate some sort of center block tend to employ it to provide adequate anchorage where necessary, allowing the use of well-secured hardware such as bridge pillars and stud tailpiece.

A semi-solid can yield some of the same sonic seasoning as a semi-acoustic, although another prime purpose behind introducing some air into the construction is to reduce the guitar's physical weight. Ever since its inception, the solidbody electric has endured criticism concerning weight, leveled by players and also many makers. With this in mind, numerous competitors to Fender and Gibson's original designs have sought to offset the inevitable increase in ounces, with makers such as G&L and Tom Anderson Guitarworks having become particularly known for their chambered designs.

There's a limit to how light wood will go and still be practical for guitar building, so the obvious solution is to incorporate some space inside the body. It's surprising how many makers have adopted this approach over the years, and with the absence of any soundholes to confirm the presence of cavities within, such semis successfully masquerade as straightforward solids, often helped by marketing that does little to alter this impression. Early so-called 'solids' from famous US names such as Gretsch, Guild, Harmony, Kay, and Rickenbacker employed degrees of hollow construction in an effort to shed pounds and make their creations more appealing, weight-wise, than those from Fender or Gibson, but of course these changes also altered tone and sustain.

Other major names flaunted the routing of a little wood from an otherwise solid body – Fender's Telecaster Thinline being perhaps the most notable – as a variation on a tested theme, appealing to players seeking only a small step toward an airier semi.

Generally, the semi suits a player who wants to hear a little more of the unplugged tone of the instrument in their amplified sound. Sure, this can sometimes introduce unwanted problems – feedback, occasional muddiness – but many guitarists are willing to overlook or overcome any drawbacks in return for the alternative aural texture of a good semi.

HYBRID DESIGNS

While the vast majority of players out there might feel that the electric guitar has evolved about as far as it needs to go – or can go – there is always that one dissenter who's looking to get something more from the instrument. It's this kind of musician who inspires designers to search for the untapped

Some semi-acoustic guitars look like solid bodied instruments, for instance this Gretsch Country Roc from 1974 (bottom left). PRS devised its hollow-bodied series of instruments in 1998; the McCarty Hollowbody II (below right) features a carved figured-maple top.

the electric guitar handbook

tone, to forge new combinations of voices, to coin a radical feature or a fresh new feel, always with one ear cocked toward the musical horizon.

Guitars generically dubbed 'hybrid' usually combine two or more means of sound reproduction for entirely new blends of tone and playability. This is more than just giving new shapes to the old familiar formulae – as did, say, Steinberger with the headless design or Floyd Rose with the locking vibrato. Typically, the new aural melange appears in the form of traditional magnetic and acoustic-like piezo pickups mounted on the same guitar; as an otherwise trad electric carrying MIDI/synth access; or simply in the form of an instrument with the look and feel of a solidbody but delivering feedback-free amplified-acoustic performance. Many also use this futuristic sonic template as a springboard for nouveau looks and radically re-thought features. The result is an ever-expanding array of makes and models that, in fairness, can hardly be categorized.

"I hate the term hybrid," says Ken Parker, who co-founded Parker Guitars with electronics expert Larry Fishman. "I build the best electric guitar I know how to make." Yet despite the objections of the man behind what is probably the best-known and defining example of the breed, it's a term the general public can latch on to. There's

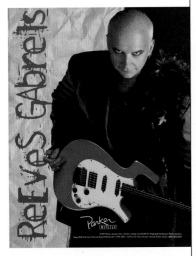

Some of the new hybrid guitars feature both magnetic and piezo pickups, including the Parker range of guitars whose press advert is shown above. The 1996 Fender catalogue announces a range of nylon-strung instruments with six-piece piezo bridge pickups (above right).

The Tom Anderson Guitarworks Hollow Drop Top from 1989 (right) has a chambered body design. The 1999 Brian Moore MC1 (far right) has a composite semi-hollow body with a solid center block and a wood top.

little doubt, however, that other visionaries in the industry share Parker's simple defining goal: "The point of the guitar is to make a guitar sound better."

By allowing the player to combine acoustic and more traditional electric sounds – all treated through the effects and amplification set-up of his or her choice – the piezo/magnetic hybrid offers near-endless nuances of color between the previously isolated primary voices of the guitar. Additionally, it offers an instant leap between the two sounds, an enormous boon for any live performer who previously had to deal with the major hassle of squeezing a dramatic electric lead break into the middle of an otherwise mellow acoustic ballad, for example. In addition to Parker, makers such as Godin, Ernie Ball/Music Man, Babicz and others have flown the flag of added sonic versatility by blending piezo and magnetic pickups in the same guitar.

Add synthesizer access to the brew and the sky's the limit sonically, though even with the improved tracking and pitch detection of newer units, the guitar synth remains an under-used musical tool.

Whatever the hardware, the new breed is earning a growing list of name users, from former Red Hot Chili Peppers and Jane's Addiction guitarist Dave Navarro to David Bowie sideman Reeves Gabrels. It's a future just beginning to reveal itself.

The Godin LG-XT from 1998 (far left) and the 1997 Parker Fly Artist (center) mixed traditional magnetic pickups with piezo units that produce a more acoustic-sounding quality. Music Man offered the option of magnetic or piezo pickups in its Axis Super Sport model from 2000 (left).

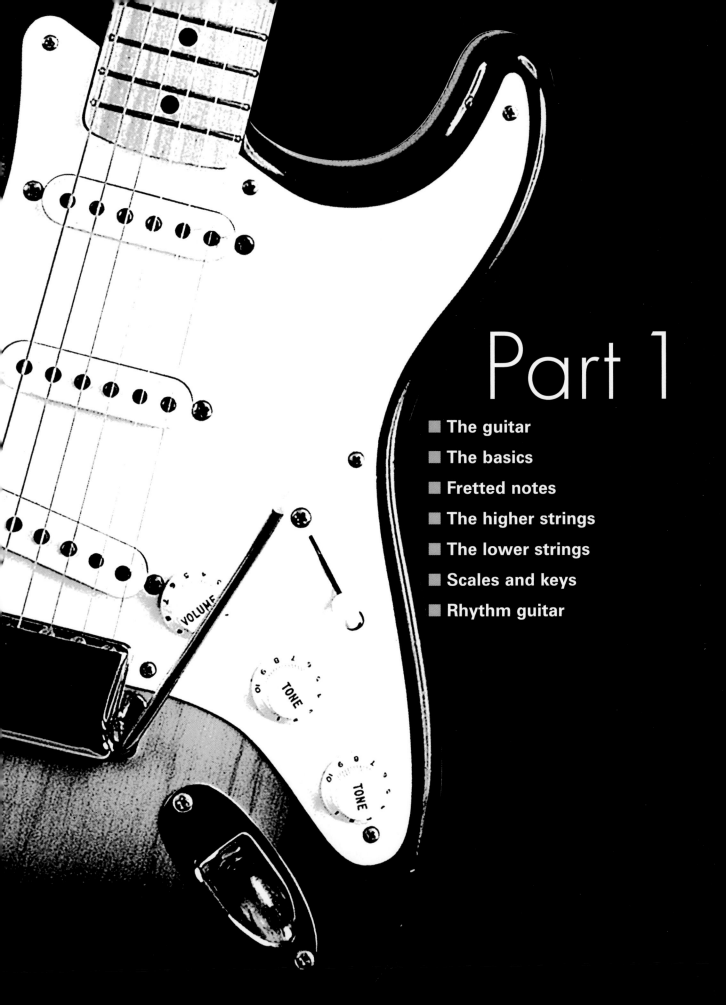

Part 1

■ the guitar

Familiarize yourself with the names of the different parts of the guitar (next page). It will help you to find your way around once we start playing some music.

THE HANDS

For most players the left hand frets the strings on the neck while the right hand plucks the strings down near the bridge. In deference to left-handed players (who often choose to do things the other way around) we shall refer in this book to fretting hand and picking hand. If you are left-handed and have not yet bought a left-handed guitar you might consider learning to play right-handed. After all, there is no such thing as a left-handed violin, a left-handed flute or, come to that, a left-handed piano. So there's no reason why one hand should necessarily be better at picking than fretting. The main advantage of learning to play right-handed is that there is a much larger range of right-handed instruments in any music store than left-handed instruments. As you progress, and wish to trade up, the choice of instruments for a right-handed player is much larger. You'll also be able to pick up any guitar and play it as if it was your own – a luxury that players of left-handed guitars have to forgo.

STANDING

When standing it's important to carry the weight of the guitar on your shoulder and across your back. A good-quality adjustable strap is essential; one that doesn't slip around is best. Don't have the strap too long; a good basic rule is that your fretting-hand wrist should be higher than its elbow. This can be a problem, as straps always seem to be made for giants. Check this before you buy.

SITTING

Practicing sitting down is less tiring than practicing standing up, and will allow you to put in the hours necessary to achieve superhero status. I recommend it very strongly. Once again it is a good idea to use a strap to keep the guitar neck up. Around a 45-degree angle is ideal. On no account should you let the neck dip below the horizontal; not only is the guitar extremely difficult to play with the neck too low, but there is also a risk of injury as you strain to get your hands in the right positions.

USING THE PICK

The examples in this book are all intended for the standard six-string electric guitar, played with a pick. The vast majority of the examples can also be effectively played on a steel-string acoustic, or even on a nylon-string classical-style guitar, and can be played fingerstyle (ie, using the fingers and thumb of the picking hand instead of a pick) if required.

the electric guitar handbook

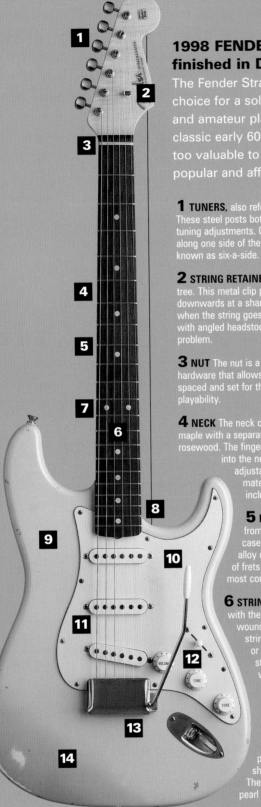

1998 FENDER RELIC 60S STRATOCASTER
finished in Daphne Blue

The Fender Stratocaster was first introduced in 1954 and has remained the first choice for a solidbodied electric guitar among a huge number of professional and amateur players. This "Relic Series" guitar is a recent faithful copy of the classic early 60s instrument. Often the originals from this period are deemed too valuable to take out on the road, which makes this particular series a popular and affordable option for players.

1 TUNERS, also referred to as machine heads. These steel posts both secure the string and allow tuning adjustments. On this guitar they are ranged along one side of the headstock; this configuration is known as six-a-side.

2 STRING RETAINER, sometimes called the string tree. This metal clip pulls the B- and top E-strings downwards at a sharper angle than might be offered when the string goes around the post. Guitars made with angled headstocks don't have this particular problem.

3 NUT The nut is a small but crucial piece of hardware that allows the six strings to be accurately spaced and set for the correct height and maximum playability.

4 NECK The neck on this instrument is cut from maple with a separate fingerboard made from rosewood. The fingerboard is glued over a slot cut into the neck to accommodate the adjustable metal truss rod. Other materials used for fingerboards include maple and ebony.

5 FRETS Fret wire can be made from a variety of materials. In this case it is made from a hardwearing alloy of nickel and silver. The number of frets on a fingerboard varies but is most commonly 22 or 24.

6 STRINGS Commonly made from nickel with the three low strings being nickel wound around a steel core. Some strings are made from stainless steel or they can be nickel plated. All strings are available in a wide variety of weights or gauges.

7 POSITION MARKERS These inlayed reference points indicate fret positions to help the players find their way around the guitar's fingerboard. These markers are plain dots, but they can be various shapes known as block markers. They are often made from mother of pearl or abalone shell.

8 NECK PLATE The neck plate is situated at the rear of the guitar where the neck joins the body. It provides a simple platform of metal through which pass the four screws that join the neck to the body. These plates often have the instrument's serial number stamped into them. Guitars with bolt-on necks have this type of fixing, but not instruments with set-in or glued-in necks.

9 BODY Materials for solidbody guitars vary widely. In this example the body is cut from a slab of alder with pre-routed holes to accommodate the pickups, wiring and controls. The slot that is cut to accept the neck is referred to as the neck pocket.

10 PICKGUARD, also known as the scratchplate. This has the function of protecting the body from plectrum strokes and covering the holes cut for the electronics. Pickguards are usually made from plastic, sometimes laminated in contrasting colors.

11 PICKUPS The pickup selector changes the sound of the guitar; each pickup sounds different because of its location. The bridge pickup sounds bright and trebly because it is near the bridge, where bright sounds predominate owing to the tightness of the string near to its anchoring point. The neck pickup sounds full and rounded because the looser string in this area accentuates the lower frequencies. Many of the musical examples suggest a pickup setting for your guitar.

12 CONTROLS The volume control adjusts how much guitar signal is going into your amplifier, and for now is probably best left on maximum as guitars usually sound best that way. Similarly the tone controls on most guitars just roll off treble and again are probably best left on maximum.

13 VIBRATO Sometimes called the tremolo, this is a bridge and/or tailpiece that alters the pitch of the strings when the arm is depressed. This unit sits on a spring-loaded block that passes through the body and returns the strings to pitch.

14 FINISH A high-gloss lacquer is used on the body. This reissue has the paintwork distressed in the factory to give it the appearance of an older used instrument. It is part of Fender's Relic Series of guitars.

TUNING

Let's start by getting your guitar in tune. There are guitar tuning notes on the CD (Track 1), but a better alternative is to buy yourself an electronic tuner. Tuners come in all shapes and sizes. They are not expensive, and some of them even clip on to the guitar and work without needing to be plugged in, which is great for acoustic. Most modern tuners recognize the string you're tuning automatically, and use a system of lights or a needle to indicate whether the string is sharp or flat. Follow each string back to its tuning peg so that you know which one to adjust – and which way to turn it to go higher (sharp) or lower (flat). At this stage it is more important to play the guitar than to tune it, so don't spend ages trying to get the tuning absolutely perfect. Spend a few minutes tuning the guitar every day, and then move on to your practicing. Your ability to tune the guitar accurately will improve with practice as we go along. If you're using an electronic tuner and you start to get erratic readings it's a sign that the battery may need replacing.

THE BASICS

Let's make a start, playing some basic guitar and understanding how guitar music is written. Have a look at the example below.

EXERCISE 1, CD TRACK 2 / Open-string notes

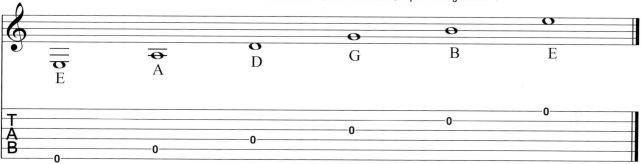

Music is written on a stave. In this case the top stave has five lines and is for standard musical notation, or 'dots' as musicians often call it. Notes can be written on the lines or in the spaces, and low or high notes that do not fit on the stave are accommodated by adding extra lines, called ledger lines. The six notes written here are the open strings of the guitar – the six sounds that the guitar makes without using the fretting hand. Beginning with the lowest sounding string, and progressing across to the highest sounding string, they are called E A D G B E. That is not particularly easy to remember at this stage, but you could try saying 'Elephants And Donkeys Grow Big Ears' and the first letter of each word will give you the name of the string. At the beginning of the stave is a 'clef'; in this case a 'treble clef' or 'G clef,' which sets the overall range of the stave by circling around the second line up and fixing that note as G.

the electric guitar handbook

For now, just repeat the names out loud as you play each note with a downstroke of the pick: E-A-D-G-B-E.

Then try playing along with the CD. The track begins with four clicks to show you when to come in, and each note lasts for four clicks. The clicks carry on in the background – you should count them 'one – two – three – four.' This introduces the idea of 'pulse' – the steady background beat that underlies virtually all music.

The lower stave has six lines and works in a completely different way. The word 'tab' at the beginning is short for tablature, and in tablature each line represents a different string of the guitar. The lowest line is your thickest, lowest sounding string. Just remember low-sounding notes are found at the bottom of the stave and high-sounding notes at the top of the stave. In tablature, an open string is notated by a zero written on the line. As we shall see when we come to play notes on the frets, which fret to play is indicated by a number written on the line.

■ THEORY

As well as being named after letters of the alphabet, the strings are numbered. Your high E-string is also called your first string, your B-string is your second string, and so on, across to your sixth string, which is your low E.

■ THEORY

In naming musical sounds we just use the first seven letters of the alphabet: A B C D E F G. Clearly there are more than seven notes on the guitar, so after G we just begin again on A. We'll return to this subject later.

EXERCISE 2, CD TRACK 3 / Counting beats

Have a listen to CD Track 3 and see Exercise 2 (opposite page). To begin with, you will hear four evenly spaced clicks. Each of these clicks is called a beat and would be written using this sign, which is called a quarter-note or crotchet:

All musicians have to count beats when they are learning music. We would count these 'one – two – three – four,' and if you look at the music you will see that it is divided up into groups of four beats by vertical lines, which are known as bar lines. In this case we have six bars of music; the word 'measure' is sometimes used instead of bar but the terms are interchangeable, and in this book we will stick to bar.

After we've finished counting our four clicks (this bit is called 'the count-in') we join in playing each open string four times. Notice this sign, which tells you to use a downstroke:

Its opposite is this sign, which tells you to use an upstroke:

V

We'll stick to downstrokes for now. The word ...*sim* means 'carry on in the same way' and saves us having to write more downstroke signs than is necessary.

At the beginning of the notation stave you will see the sign that looks like this:

4
4

This is called the time signature, and it tells us that this piece is in 4/4, meaning there are four quarter-notes in every bar. Of course, in this case we knew that already – but there are not always four beats in a bar, and this sign can warn us what to expect.

■ THEORY

Once we start grouping beats together in patterns of strong or weak beats we move beyond 'pulse' and begin dealing with 'meter.' A pulse is a steady even beat, whereas a meter has a regular louder or accented beat as the first of each group. Four is the most common meter and is the one used for most popular music, but you could have any number of beats per bar.

In 'Open Season' (next page) we are using the top three open strings of the guitar to play a melody. Remember: 'top three' means 'three highest sounding.' We are also introducing some new signs and some work for the left-hand. Firstly this sign is called a 'rest,' and has the same duration as a quarter-note or crotchet:

PRO TIP

In music, terms like 'low' and 'high' always refer to the pitch of the music. So the 'low' end of the guitar is near the nut, on the first few frets, where the lowest notes are found. If you read 'go up one fret' it means 'go one fret higher in pitch.' This would mean moving your hand in a downwards direction, nearer to the floor. It's the same with strings: your low E-string is nearest the ceiling, and your high E-string is nearest the floor. Get used to these terms now or you will find some of the coming explanations confusing. Just remember that low and high always refer to pitch.

the electric guitar handbook

THE GUITAR

EXERCISE 3, **CD TRACK 4** / 'Open Season'

A rest is a musical term for a silence. The best way to 'play' a silence in this case is to mute the guitar strings by laying the left-hand fingers flat across all six strings of the guitar. Using the left hand to silence the guitar in this way is good for your coordination and will help when we start using the fingers to play notes on the frets.

There is also a new type of note, which is called a half-note or minim and lasts for two beats:

A half-note rest would look like this:

As the time signature is again 4/4, or four quarter-notes per bar, there can't be more than two half-notes in a bar. If you're counting four beats in the bar (as you should be), these notes will fall on beat one and beat three. Notice that the tail (or stem) of the note can go up or down – it's the type of note that matters.

The tab just consists of zeros to tell you to play open strings, whereas the notation stave has different note types to tell you what rhythm to play and different pitches depending on the note's position on the stave. Go through the piece before you play it, saying the letter names of the notes you are about to play. Learning to read letter names is one of the two fundamental skills of learning to read music. (The other is learning to read rhythm.)

the electric guitar handbook

EXERCISE 4, CD TRACK 5 / The D-string

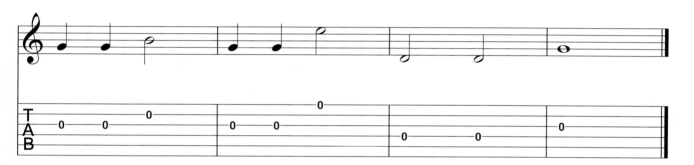

■ THEORY

It is possible to write rhythm on a tab stave, but when tab is combined with standard notation the rhythms are normally omitted from the tab stave to avoid unnecessary duplication. So read your rhythms from the notation stave, and read your notes from the tab – or even better, read the whole thing using just the notation stave.

Now that you're reading and playing notes on the top three open strings, it's time to add another string – the D-string. In Exercise 4 (above) we are also testing your pick technique, by jumping from string to string more often, and your counting, by mixing up half-notes and quarter-notes. You should still be counting 'one – two – three – four' in each bar. If you look at the first bar, you will see that the first note, G, should be played as you say 'one'; the next note, B, should be played as you say 'three'; and the last note of the bar, G, should be played as you say 'four.' In bar four, you will see a new kind of note, called a whole-note or semibreve, which lasts for four beats – filling the whole bar of 4/4. It looks like this:

A whole-note rest looks like this:

PRO TIP

Once again we are just using downstrokes with the pick. Just as an experiment, put the pick down and try playing the piece using just your pick-hand thumb. You will find you have to do a downstroke, and you will probably produce a different sound from the guitar. You can rest your fingers on the front of the guitar for stability if you want to.

the electric guitar handbook

Try counting your way through the piece and clapping your hands each time you should play a note. When you're confident with that, have a listen to the CD track and play along on your guitar. At the end of the piece you can see this sign, called a repeat sign:

It tells you to go back to the beginning of the piece and play it again. On the CD track, only the backing track is repeated, leaving you to play the melody on your own (a solo!) second time through.

■ THEORY

You may have noticed that each piece of music ends with a final bar line that looks like this, whether there's a repeat sign or not:

 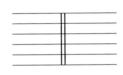

We also sometimes use a double bar line to mark the end of a section within a larger piece. It looks like this (left).

EXERCISE 5, CD TRACK 6 / 'The Low Down'

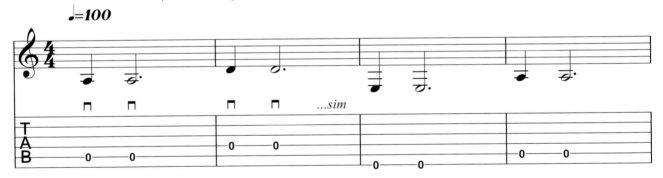

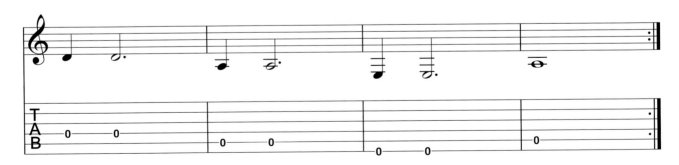

So far we have seen the quarter-note, which lasts one beat, a half-note, which lasts two beats, and a whole-note, which lasts four beats. Exercise 5 introduces the dotted half-note, which lasts three beats:

$\sf{\it d.}$

In fact, any note or rest can be dotted, and the function of the dot is to lengthen the note by half its value. So the two-beat half-note is lengthened to three beats. A dotted whole-note would be worth six beats, but you won't see one very often. A dotted quarter-note would last one-and-a-half beats. We'll discuss how you can have half a beat in a later example.

In terms of notes, this example concentrates on the lowest three strings of the guitar, again just using open strings. Count the four beats in each bar, playing only on beats one and two, and letting the second note (the dotted half-note) ring for beats two, three, and four. As before, the piece is repeated, allowing you to take over on the second time through.

■ THEORY

You might have noticed at the start of the piece there is this sign:

$\sf{\it J}$=100

This is a metronome mark, which tells you how fast the piece of music is to be played. In this case, there should be 100 quarter-notes per minute. This is known as the 'BPM' or beats per minute. If you have a metronome you could set it clicking at exactly the right speed for the example.

This brings us to the end of the first section – Basics – of Part One. Let's recap what we've learned in this chapter: the names of parts of the guitar; the importance of posture; tuning; music and tablature staves; time signatures; the names of the open strings and how they are written; counting beats; quarter-notes and rests; pick directions; half-notes, whole-notes, and rests; repeat signs; dotted notes and metronome marks; and reading the open strings on the notation stave.

If you're puzzled by anything on this list, check back to the relevant section and hopefully things will become clearer.

Now we're moving on to notes on the frets.

the electric guitar handbook

fretted notes

We're going to move on from playing the open strings to playing notes on the frets.

I'd like you to play your highest-sounding open string, (which we know produces the note E) and listen to how it sounds. Now take the index finger of your fretting hand (for most people this will be your left hand) and press the same string down against the first fret. Your finger should be as close to the fret as it can be without being on top of it. If you play the string again you will hear that the pitch has changed. What was originally an open E is now a fretted F. Your fretting-hand thumb should be opposite your finger on the back of the neck and you should squeeze between the thumb and the tip of your index finger just enough to hold the string down. Your shoulders, elbows, and wrists should be relaxed. Do not hunch over the guitar.

The fingers of the fretting hand are numbered from one to four, starting with the index finger and ending with the little finger or pinky. Rule one of using the fretting hand is to use one finger per fret. So now I'd like you to play the second fret with your second finger, third fret with your third finger and fourth fret with your fourth finger. Rule two of using the fretting hand is that you should use the tips of your fingers, so the tip-joints of your fingers should be more or less pointing straight at the guitar. (There is some leeway here depending on the size and shape of your hand, but it's definitely something to aim for.) That's enough rules for now – try to keep them in mind.

EXERCISE 6 / First string fretted notes

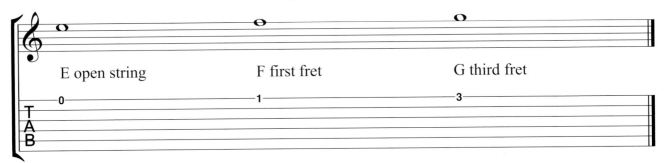

Now let's learn some new notes. We already know that the first string produces the note E, which is written in the top space on the stave. If we play the note on the first fret on that string we produce an F, which is written on the top line of the stave. If we play the note on the third fret we produce the note G, which is written above the stave. Notice that the tablature stave now has a 1 on the top line beneath the F; this tells you to play the first fret on the first string. Under the G there is a 3 on the top line, which tells you to play the third fret.

Using our two new notes we are going to play 'First String Thing.' This piece uses quarter-notes, half-notes, and whole-notes, and there are four beats in the bar. All the notes are E, F, or G; open string, first fret, or third fret on your first string. This time there is no repeat – just play along with the CD. Remember the one finger per fret rule?

EXERCISE 7, CD TRACK 7 / 'First String Thing'

You should be using your index finger (finger one) to play F and finger three to play G. If you have small hands and the stretch to finger three is difficult, it's a good idea at this stage to use finger four at the third fret. Don't jump in and listen to the CD track before you've given yourself a chance to go through the piece clapping the rhythm while you count the beats. Then go through the piece reading the notation stave and saying the letter names out loud as you play them. You should now be ready to play the example along with the CD track.

■ THEORY

You might have noticed that you now have two notes called G. If you play them both and let them ring on you should hear that the higher G seems to get lost in the lower open string G; essentially, they sound 'the same but different.' The gap between these two notes is called an octave, as the high G is the eighth letter-name above the lower G. We first came across notes with the same letter-name when we learned the names of the open strings; we have two E-strings, the sixth string and the first string, but in that case they are two octaves apart.

G	A	B	C	D	E	F	G
1	2	3	4	5	6	7	8

Staying with notes on the first string for the time being, we're going to try a piece with a different time signature. Exercise 8 is in three-four time (3/4), which means you will count three quarter-notes or crotchets in each bar. In this time signature a dotted half-note fills the whole bar. If you can get your head around the different counting this piece is not much harder than the previous example. Once again, you should begin by clapping the rhythm while counting the beats (remember just count 'one – two – three' and not 'four') and then making sure you can say the letter names out loud. Do it this way and you will be well on the way to learning to read music.

■ THEORY

At the end of this piece you will see two open E notes joined together with a curving line. This is called a 'tie,' and it means that instead of re-picking the second note you just let the first note ring on. In other words, it adds the second note to the first to create a long note that in this case is six beats long. A tie is useful as it is the only way we can write a note that is longer than one bar. As we will see, sometimes a tie is also used in the middle of a bar. Notice that the second E is not shown in the tablature as it is not actually picked.

PRO TIP

Is your playing 'legato'? Legato is an Italian word meaning 'joined up,' and in music we take it to mean there are no silences between the notes. On guitar it's possible to be so busy playing the note at the right time that we forget to listen to whether it lasts as long as it should. So play joined-up notes (legato), not separated notes (which are called 'staccato').

FRETTED NOTES

EXERCISE 8, CD TRACK 8 / Introducing 3/4

the electric guitar handbook

It's time to learn some more new notes. Earlier on, I told you that musical sounds are named after the first seven letters of the alphabet. This is true, and the letters ABCDEFG would be the white notes on a keyboard. If you look at a keyboard, you will notice that between most of the white notes there are black notes. These are the flats and sharps.

The sign for a flat is: ♭

The sign for a sharp is: ♯

This illustration shows the note names for one octave of a keyboard. All the other octaves have the same note names.

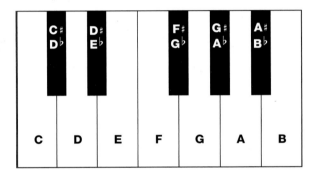

We've started on C only because of musical convention; we could have started on any note. Notice that not every note has a sharp or flat; there is no black note between B and C, or between E and F. This is why, when you play the open E string, the next note up is F at the first fret, whereas there is a two fret gap between F and G, leaving room for F-sharp at the second fret.

So now we know that the letter names A to G are the white notes of the keyboard, and the sharps and flats are the black notes. Let's check that we know where these black notes are on the guitar.

We've already met the notes E, F, and G on the first string. F is on the first fret, G

EXERCISE 9 / Introducing F-sharp

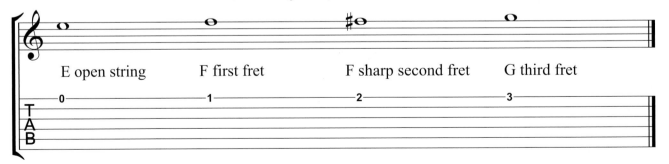

is on the third fret. F-sharp (F♯) or G-flat (G♭) is found on the second fret, as we can see from this example. For now, let's stick to calling our new note F-sharp, but get used to the idea that a note can have two names.

■ THEORY

When a sharp or a flat occurs during a piece of music it is called an 'accidental.'

Let's play 'Blues One,' which uses F-sharp along with the other notes we've learnt on the E string. This time we will also add the open B-string. Can you remember which one is your B-string? Go back to Section One and check it out if not.

Before we play this piece we need to learn one more thing about flats and sharps.

EXERCISE 10, CD TRACK 9 / 'Blues One'

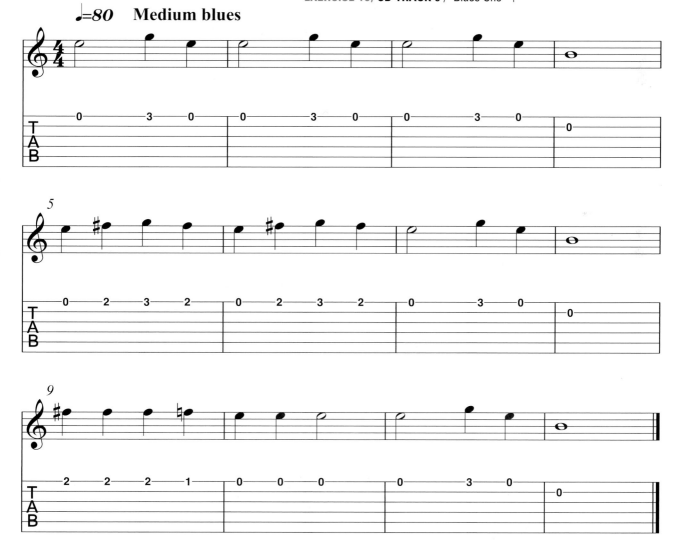

FRETTED NOTES

Once you have a sharp or flat in a bar it affects all the notes of that pitch in that bar. Take a look at bar five. You will see that the second note, F, is preceded by a sharp, so we know that note is F-sharp. But as the sharp lasts for the whole bar, the F at the end of the bar is also sharp. So what do we do if we want to start with F-sharp and then have a normal F? We use a 'natural' sign:

A natural cancels a flat or sharp. Take a look at bar nine. This begins with three F-sharps, but the fourth F is a normal F, or 'F-natural' as we would say.

■ THEORY

There's one other new thing in Exercise 10. Next to the metronome mark it says 'Medium blues.' This is the place where a composer will write a few words to tell you something about the style of the piece of music. 'Medium' in this case refers to the speed, and 'blues' gives you an idea of the feel of the piece. In classical music, composers often use Italian terms like 'allegro' (fast) or 'moderato' (medium) instead of the metronome mark.

Now that we've covered sharps and flats let's move on to learning notes on the B-string. Here they are:

EXERCISE 11 / B-string notes

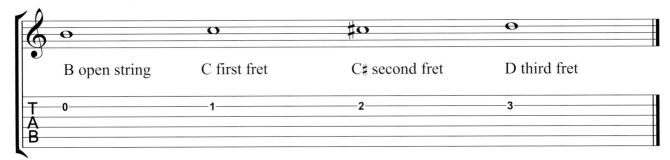

Once again we are going to play a tune using these new notes, and we are going to stay with the blues for 'Blues Two.'

Make sure you know the names of the new notes we've learnt on the B-string; saying the letter names aloud as you read music is the best way to do this. Since there are notes on both the B-string and the E-string in this piece you may find the odd slip-up as you cross over between the strings. This is because you are doing one kind of movement with your pick hand and another kind with your fret hand. Be patient and play the music more slowly than on the CD until you've mastered the coordination needed to play this piece.

PRO TIP

If you listen to this piece of music you will notice that it has phrases similar to those found in everyday speech. The first four bars make up one phrase, the next four bars another phrase, and the final four bars another, making three phrases in all. If you need to break this piece down into smaller sections to make it easier to learn, try playing it one phrase at a time.

the electric guitar handbook

EXERCISE 12, CD TRACK 10 / 'Blues Two'

♩=80 **Medium blues**

■ THEORY

Have you memorized the names of these signs?

♭ = flat ♯ = sharp ♮ = natural

All of the music we've played so far has used quarter-notes (crotchets), half-notes (minims), or whole-notes (semibreves), and we are used to the idea of one beat being a quarter-note. When we wish to play shorter notes, for example, two notes to a beat, we use eighth-notes (quavers):

PRO TIP

Keep your fret-hand fingers pointing at the strings all the time. When you release your fingers from holding down the strings, don't let them pop up too far from the neck; aim to keep your fingers a half-inch or quarter-inch from the strings so that they are ready to play the next note.

the electric guitar handbook

EXERCISE 13, CD TRACK 11 / Upstrokes and downstrokes

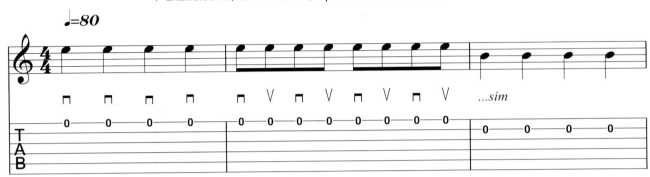

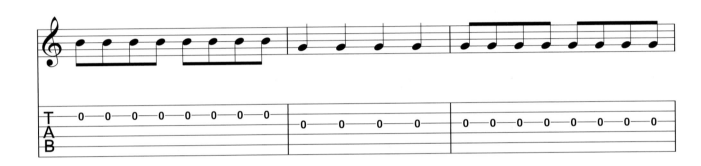

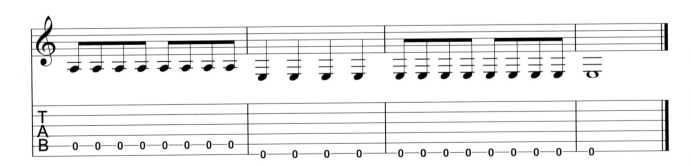

Playing eighth-notes gives us an opportunity to start using upstrokes with the pick. Here's the upstroke symbol again:

In this example, we begin with four quarter-note downstrokes on the first string and then go to eighth-notes, alternating downstrokes and upstrokes. We work our way across the guitar playing all the open strings in turn. Count the quarter-notes 'one – two – three – four' and count the eighth-notes 'one-and two-and three-and four-and.' This track has a two-bar count-in.

■ THEORY

A single eighth-note is written like this:

When there are several eighth-notes they can be joined together like this:

If you have memorized the names of the notes on the E-string and B-string you won't have any problem reading 'Blues Three' (next page). When it comes to counting the rhythm, however, you will need to say 'and' in between each beat to get the eighth-notes right. As we said above, when you have quarter-notes, you count 'one – two – three – four' and when eighth-notes are present you count 'one-and two-and three-and four-and.' So bar one would be 'one two-and three four.' The count is given underneath the first few bars.

You've probably started to realize that reading tablature is very easy, particularly when you have a CD track to listen to. However, without any rhythm notation it would be very hard to get the tablature right if you hadn't heard the piece first. Reading music notation, on the other hand, requires you to memorize the note names as they appear on the stave and their locations on the guitar, and also to learn to read rhythms. While this is much harder to do, it also makes it possible for you to play music accurately even if you have never heard before. Remember, even if you're hurrying through these exercises using only the tablature, you can always come back later and use them to learn to read music.

PRO TIP

When they first start out, many players make bigger movements with the pick than they need to. Point the pick straight at the guitar and move it from side to side keeping it close to the strings; let your hand move lightly from the wrist.

EXERCISE 14, CD TRACK 12 / 'Blues Three'

Let's move on to the first three frets on the G-string now. Here they are:

EXERCISE 15 / G-string notes

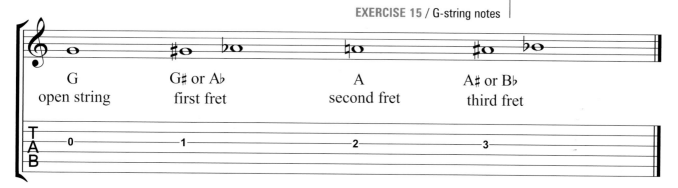

'Blues Four' (next page) uses these new notes and the notes on the B-string and E-string that we have learned already.

This is the last blues for a while - it's a simple one rhythmically but it does cross from the G-string right over to the E-string, testing your ability to land your fret-hand finger on the right note just as you pick the string.

We've reached the stage where we now know most of the names of the notes on the first three strings of the guitar. To keep things simple we've concentrated on the first three frets. Since you have four fingers it might be a good idea at this point to extend your knowledge to include the fourth fret. This also gives us the chance to revise the notes we've already learnt.

PRO TIP

You are probably trying to look at your fret hand while you play, and possibly your pick hand too. Clearly, it is difficult to do both; and looking at the music at the same time is completely impossible. The secret is to feel your way around the guitar and not look at your hands at all. If you try this, you may well slip up a little at first, but if you persevere you will eventually be able to read music as you play. Keeping your eyes on the music is a skill you must develop if you wish to learn to sight-read; this is what we call it when you can read a new piece of music on your instrument without puzzling it out first.

EXERCISE 16, **CD TRACK 13** / 'Blues Four'

Here are the notes for the first four frets on the top three strings:

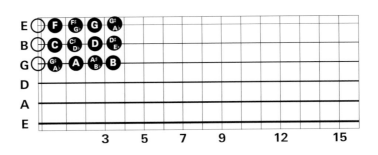

FRETTED NOTES

EXERCISE 17 / Top three string notes

First or E string:

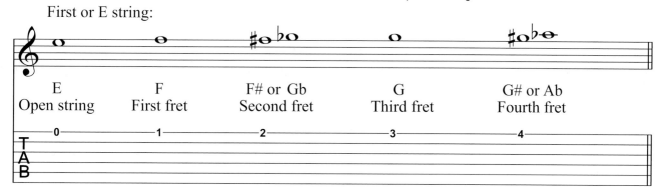

E	F	F# or Gb	G	G# or Ab
Open string	First fret	Second fret	Third fret	Fourth fret

Second or B string:

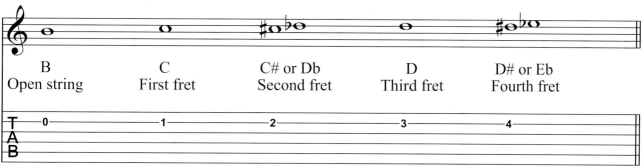

B	C	C# or Db	D	D# or Eb
Open string	First fret	Second fret	Third fret	Fourth fret

Third or G string:

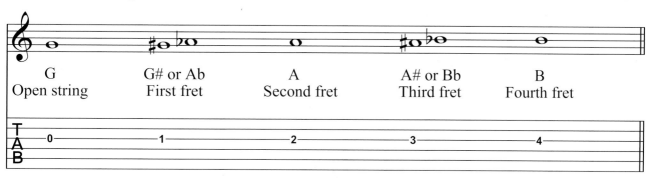

G	G# or Ab	A	A# or Bb	B
Open string	First fret	Second fret	Third fret	Fourth fret

Notice that as you work your way up the G-string you come to B at the fourth fret. This is the same note as your open B-string, so in future you could play this note instead of an open B if you want to. This also introduces the idea that virtually every note on the guitar is available in several different places. We will return to the subject of choosing where to play any given note later.

the electric guitar handbook

FRETTED NOTES

Playing all the notes, including the sharps and flats, produces a scale known as a chromatic scale. Chromatic means colorful. We are going to play a one-octave chromatic scale starting on your open G-string. As we don't need to play the note B twice, we will only need the first three frets on the G-string, four frets on the B-string, and then the first three frets on the E-string to take us up to the octave G. Here it is:

EXERCISE 18, CD TRACK 14 / One-octave chromatic scale

There are many different kinds of scale in music, some of which can be very useful to the guitar player, as they are used for making up riffs and solos. This scale is useful mainly as a finger exercise and also for showing where notes are on the guitar. Notice that for convenience we have used sharps going up and flats on the way back down, which saves us from having to use naturals. Use one finger for each fret, and 'alternate picking' with your pick hand. Alternate picking is the commonest and most dependable pick-hand technique of all. Simply follow each downstroke with an upstroke as indicated in the music. Because scales are technically straightforward to play they can be very useful for practicing pick technique.

■ THEORY

The notation stave in this example includes small numbers written next to the notes. This is known as 'fingering' and tells you which fret-hand finger to use; 1 is your index finger, 4 is your pinky. Guitar music, especially classical guitar, will often include fingerings.

PRO TIP

Try playing all of these notes in turn from your open G-string all the way up to the third fret on the E-string and see if you can name them. This is the best way to learn the guitar note names. Say them in full: G, G-sharp or A-flat, A, A-sharp or B-flat, etc.

the electric guitar handbook

To round off this section we are going to play 'Shadow Walk,' a surf-style piece that uses all the notes we've learnt so far. 'Surf' suggests the twangy guitar music of the 1960s, but it is mixed in here with some of the melodic style of The Shadows' Hank Marvin. Use the bridge pickup on your guitar and set up a clean, bright sound on your amp. Add a little reverb and a fluttering delay (echo) effect if you have them. Hank would probably have used a Binson Echorec or similar mechanical delay unit.

EXERCISE 19, CD TRACK 15 / 'Shadow Walk'

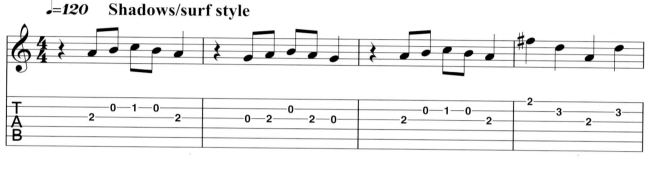

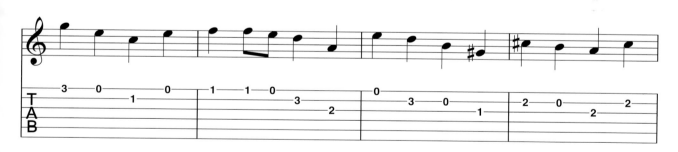

continued over page

the electric guitar handbook

FRETTED NOTES

EXERCISE 19, **CD TRACK 15** / 'Shadow Walk' *continued*

This example uses lots of eighth-notes and moves around from the G-string to the E-string and right up to the fourth fret. There are also some quarter-note rests, and the piece is much longer than most of the examples we've looked at so far. Don't be surprised if it takes a while to get to grips with the whole thing. We'll tackle the rhythm part when we get to Part Two.

In this section we have covered the following: more advanced counting in 4/4 time; note reading on the first, second, and third strings; sharps and flats; octaves; tempo and style; phrases; and much of the basic technique of guitar playing. Hopefully you're becoming more confident with the names of the notes and where they are on the guitar.

Going forward into the next section, remember to make small movements with the fret-hand fingers, keeping them close to the guitar and using your fingertips. Don't squeeze any tighter than you need to and use your thumb to press gently at the back of the neck. Try to relax any bits of you not actually used for playing the guitar (neck, shoulders, elbows, wrists, etc). You'll be amazed how much unnecessary tension you can build up. As for the pick hand, from now on we will use alternate pick-strokes and you should aim to make small, relaxed movements with the pick.

PRO TIP

It's a good idea to break a long piece down into shorter sections for learning purposes. Try playing four bars at a time; that is usually enough to absorb in one go, and, as we've seen, music very often uses four-bar phrases.

the electric guitar handbook

the lower strings

Now we are going to move on to learning notes on the lower three strings of the guitar. Remember 'lower' means 'lowest sounding.'

These three strings (the E, A, and D strings) are sometimes called the bass strings, with the highest three strings being called the treble strings. Let's start with the D or fourth string. Here are the notes on this new string:

EXERCISE 20 / D-string notes

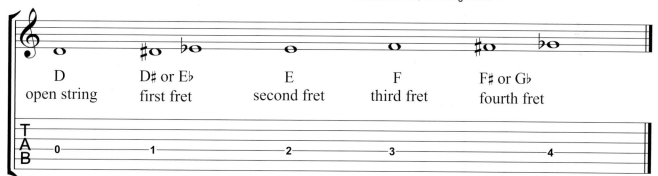

Notice that we go straight from E at the second fret to F at the third fret; as we've seen before, there is no sharp between E and F. Play these notes one by one saying each letter name and using one finger per fret.

Exercise 21 (next page) is a groovy swamp-rock tune that uses notes on the D-string together with those we have already learned on the G-string.

When you listen to the track you will hear that there is an effect on the guitar part. This is called tremolo. It is a rhythmic fluctuation in volume that was often an integral part of the sound of classic valve amplifiers in the 1950s and 1960s. Usually, you have speed and depth (or intensity) controls, and you adjust the speed control so that the fluctuation pulses in time with the music. Nowadays, it is often found in effect pedals, but don't worry if you don't have anything like it – just play the piece anyway. Use the neck pickup of your guitar to make a fat tone; on the CD track you can hear a touch of overdrive too.

Now take a look at the first bar of the example. You might be worried to see that there are some notes missing. There seem to be only three eighth-notes in this bar. This is because not all music starts on the first beat of the bar. In this case you have to count one, two, three beats and then play the last three eighth-notes of the bar,

the electric guitar handbook

THE LOWER STRINGS

EXERCISE 21, **CD TRACK 16** / 'Swamp Thing'

♩=90 **Swamp rock**

With slow tremolo effect throughout...

the electric guitar handbook

counting 'and four-and.' There will be seven clicks at the start of this piece, four of which are the usual one-bar count in, with three more giving you the missing beats from this incomplete bar.

At the end of the piece, just before the repeat sign, you will see a bar with the number 1 written above it inside a bracket:

<pre>
┌────────────┐
│ 1.   │
</pre>

We call this the 'first-time bar' and after playing this bar we go back to the repeat sign at the beginning. Second time through, you've already played the first-time bar so you go straight to the second-time bar, which has the number 2 written above it:

<pre>
┌────────────┐
│ 2.   │
</pre>

This lets us have two different endings; the first leads into a repeat, and the second leads to the end.

■ THEORY

As this piece is written mostly in eighth-notes, you will be counting 'one-and two-and three-and four-and.' Remember to make your quarter-notes twice as long as your eighth-notes. You will be seeing some of this sign, which is an eighth-note rest:

𝄾

(You remember rests? A rest is a silence.)

Let's move on to the A-string. First, here are the notes:

EXERCISE 22 / A-string notes

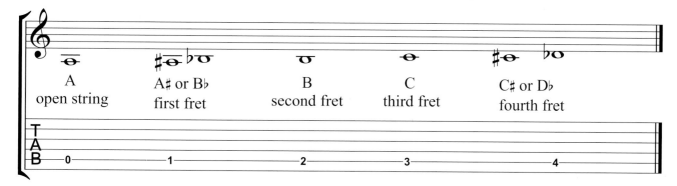

You know the drill by now; say the letter names out loud as you play these notes, using one finger on each fret.

PRO TIP

Aim to play this piece using both downstrokes and upstrokes with the pick. Use downstrokes on the downbeats (that's beats one, two, three, and four) and upstrokes on the 'and' in between.

THE LOWER STRINGS

EXERCISE 23, **CD TRACK 17** / 'Defective Detective'

♩=*100*   **1960s TV detective theme**

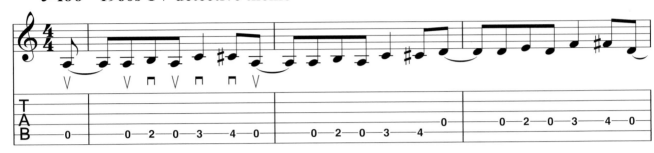

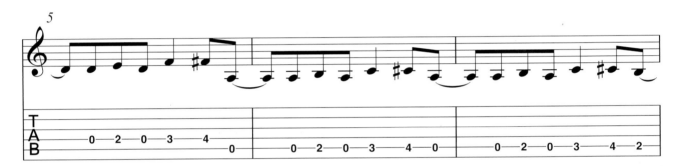

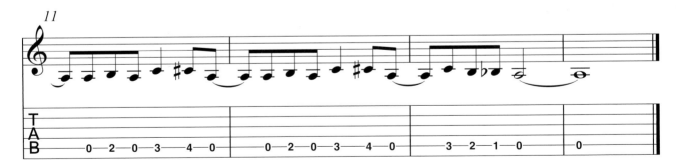

the electric guitar handbook

'Defective Detective' (Exercise 23) concentrates on notes on the A-string, but also includes some of the notes we've just learnt on the D-string.

Once again we begin before the first beat of the bar; in this case, on the very last eighth-note. Notice the ties across the bar lines. We are playing on 'and' but holding the note across the first beat 'one.' Normally the first beat is accented (ie, played more strongly) but in this case the accent falls in front of the first beat. This shifting of accents is an essential part of the style of rock, blues, jazz, and all related types of music. It's known as syncopation.

■ THEORY

Musicians use a variety of names for an incomplete bar at the start of the piece of music. The technical name for it is an 'anacrusis.' Rock musicians are more likely to call it an 'upbeat' or a 'lead-in.'

We've finally reached the E or sixth string. Once you play this exercise you will have played all the notes on the guitar in what is known as the first position. First, let's learn the notes.

EXERCISE 24 / E-string notes

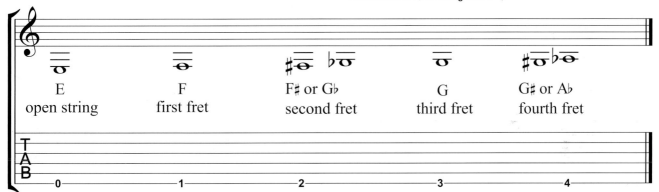

■ THEORY

Where you are on the guitar is often described in terms of 'positions.' If your first finger is at the first fret and you are playing on frets one to four, you are in the first position. If your first finger is on the second fret, and you are playing frets two to five you would be in the second position, and so on.

PRO TIP

Use a clean biting tone from your bridge pickup, and start with an upstroke, following the picking pattern that's given in the first bar. This should let you keep the downstrokes on the downbeats. Play with lots of attitude; imagine you've been booked for a recording session back in the 1960s, and you're playing the theme tune of a big new detective series.

EXERCISE 25, CD TRACK 18 / 'E-string Boogie'

♩=80   **Slow boogie**

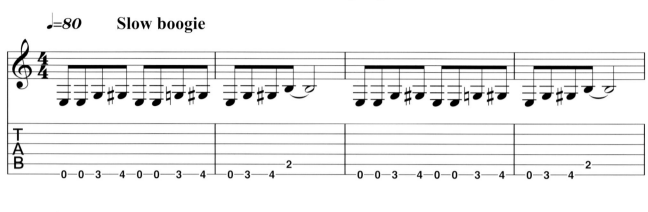

In Exercise 25 we once again have a piece that uses all these new notes, along with some we've come across before. From the music-reading point of view, there are a great many ledger lines and it can all get a bit confusing. The trick is to remember that there are only six letter names on the guitar that use ledger lines below the stave. These notes are: E, F, and G on the sixth string, and A, B, and C on the fifth string. Once you learn the position of the six notes on the stave it all gets much easier and you just have to deal with any flats and sharps that come along.

In this piece we have ties in the middle of the bar. An eighth-note tied to a half-note makes a note which is two-and-a-half beats long. Using a tie helps with counting the rhythm, as it allows us to see the middle of the bar where the third beat begins. Make sure you give these tied notes their full value when you play the piece. In this example we need a thick, bassy tone; use your middle or neck pickup and add a touch of distortion from your amp or from an effects box if you have it.

PRO TIP

The steady eighth-note movement of this piece is a great opportunity to work on your alternate picking. Start each phrase with a downstroke and carry on alternating downstrokes and upstrokes. If you find it difficult, try it a little more slowly, but hang in there and persevere. Alternate picking is the most dependable and versatile way of playing single notes on the guitar – it's the 'industry standard.'

The next example (Exercise 26) gets you playing music across all the lower strings of the guitar. There are several new ingredients added on the notation stave. Firstly, this is the first time we've seen a dotted quarter-note. We know that a dot adds half a note's value, so our quarter-note is worth one-and-a-half beats when dotted. That's the same as a quarter-note plus an eighth-note. The second note of the bar is an eighth-note tied to a quarter-note; this is also one-and-a-half beats long, but the use of the tie here lets us see where the third beat begins, hopefully making the music easier to read. The count is given underneath the first bar to make this clearer.

THE LOWER STRINGS

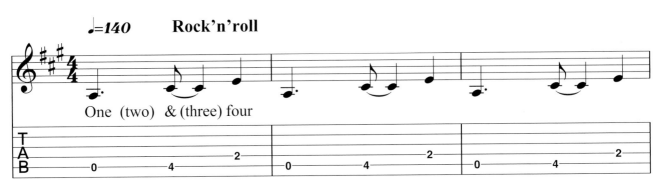

One (two) & (three) four

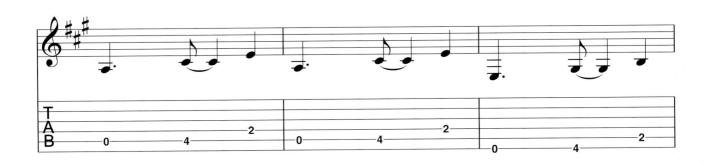

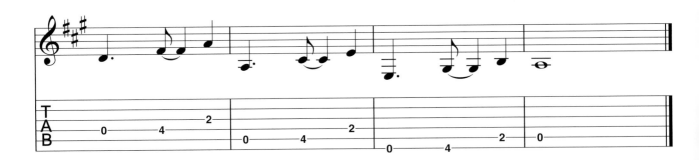

the electric guitar handbook

If you look at the very start of each line you will see three sharps on the notation stave: F-sharp, C-sharp, and G-sharp. Sharps and flats in this position on the stave are known as a key signature. Every F, C, and G in this piece is played sharp, and providing you can remember this, writing the sharps at the beginning of the stave makes the music look a lot less cluttered; you no longer need so many sharps in each bar. The key signature also has another function; to tell us what key we are in. The keynote in music is like a home note; the place the music wants to come home to. The three sharps give us the key of A major and the music begins and ends on the note A. We will return to keys and key signatures later.

■ THEORY

This piece is based around a repeated pattern of notes, which musicians would normally call a 'riff.' Sometimes the word riff is used to mean 'a musical idea' which need not necessarily be repeated. In this piece the riff is based on the three notes that make up a chord of A major (A, C-sharp, and E). Then the riff is shifted up to D major (D, F-sharp, and A) and finally E major (E, G-sharp, and B). We take a closer look at chord construction in Part Two.

EXERCISE 27 / All notes to fifth fret

the electric guitar handbook

Exercise 27 shows the notes we've learnt so far in the first position, but also includes notes at the fifth fret. The fifth fret is the point at which most of the notes of the guitar begin to overlap. At the fifth fret on the low E-string we have the note A, the same pitch as the next open string. At the fifth fret on the A-string, we have the note D, the next open string, and so on. The odd one out is the G-string, which has the note B at the fourth fret. Here they are as a fingerboard diagram.

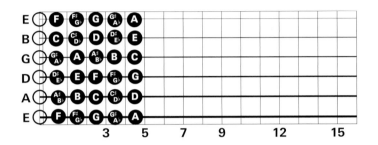

PRO TIP

When it comes to fingering, you should use finger four at the fourth fret, and finger two at the second fret. You might like to try using finger three at the fourth fret and finger one at the second fret – it seems to fit the hand better this way. Technically you'd then be playing in the second position. If in the future you take a look at some classical guitar music, you may see position markers in the music as Roman numerals above the stave.

FIFTH-FRET TUNING

Now that we know where the notes on the guitar overlap, we have the chance to tune the guitar a different way. Up to now, you have used either the tuning notes on the CD or an electronic tuner if you have one. An alternative would be to play the note on the fifth fret of the E-string and tune the open A to the same pitch. Then play the fifth fret on the A-string (the note D) and tune the open D to match. Continue in the same way, using the fifth fret on the D-string to produce the pitch of the open G, the fourth fret on the G to produce the open B, and finally the fifth fret on the B-string to produce the open E. This is usually called 'fifth-fret tuning' and is worth knowing about in case you ever forget your tuner or its battery goes flat.

Now that we have all the notes on the guitar up to the fifth fret, here is a metal-style piece that is played on the first string of the guitar and uses the note A at the fifth fret. If you put your first finger at the second fret you will be in the second position; using one finger per fret you will be able to reach the fifth fret with your pinky. So for your fret hand the whole piece can be played with fingers one, two, and four.

PRO TIP

Watch out for the picking symbols. We have downstrokes on the downbeats and upstrokes on the upbeats. It's not a law but it works out best most of the time. We will be returning to this piece in the future to learn the rhythm guitar part.

■ THEORY

You often find chord symbols written under the stave in guitar music. Here we have chords of E5, B5, C5 etc. These tell you what's going on in the other guitar part. Don't worry if you don't know what they mean just yet – we'll make a start on chords later in this section.

EXERCISE 28, **CD TRACK 20** / 'Movable Metal'

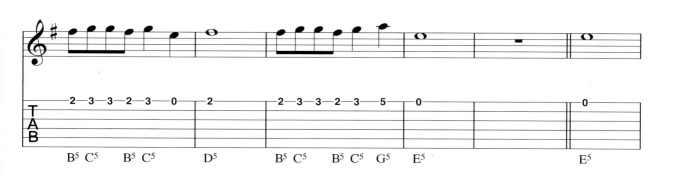

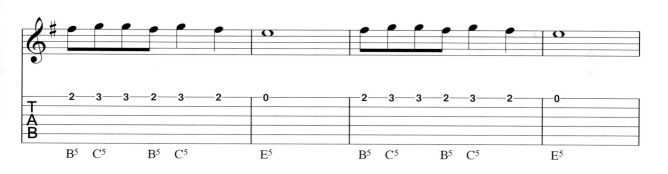

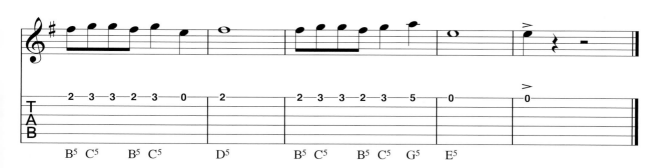

the electric guitar handbook

THE LOWER STRINGS

EXERCISE 29, CD track 21 / 'John Lee'

♩=105 **Blues**

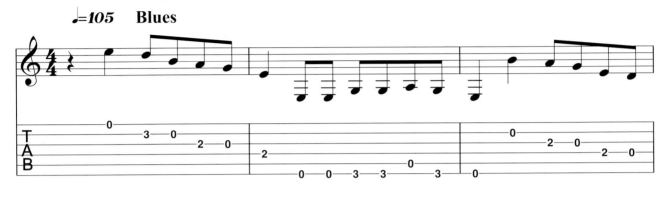

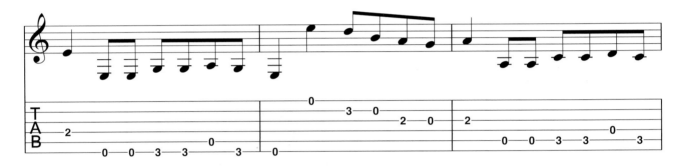

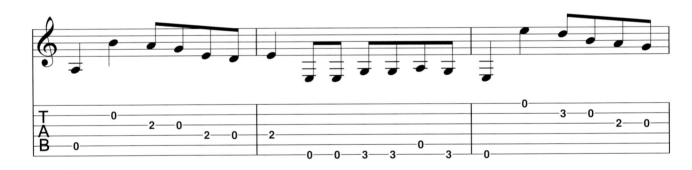

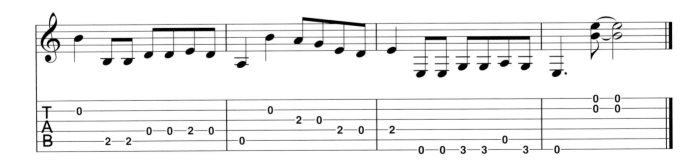

the electric guitar handbook

Exercise 29 has a very wide range, from the lowest notes on the bottom string to the open high E-string. It is inspired by the great blues legend John Lee Hooker, and uses a call and response structure in which the high notes ask a question and the low notes provide the answer.

Probably the hardest part of this piece will be dealing with the pick technique, which involves crossing the strings in bigger leaps than before. Take it slowly, and if possible learn to do it without looking at your pick hand. In the long run you'll be glad you did! Notice that there is a rest on the first beat of the bar and the music begins on the second beat.

EXERCISE 30, CD TRACK 22 / Blues scale in E

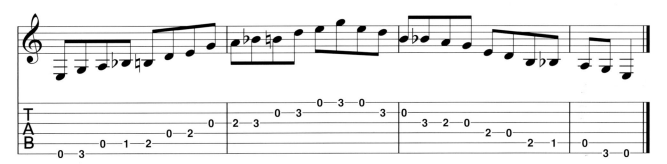

Now we are going to learn a new scale. Not just any scale – this is the blues scale. The piece above, Exercise 29, is based entirely upon this scale, as are several other examples we've already come across in the book. When it comes to playing guitar solos or making up riffs, the blues scale is king. You will hear its sounds all over rock music, in riffs and grooves everywhere, from the earliest days of blues and rock'n'roll, through classic rock and heavy metal, onwards to soul and dance music and up to the present day. So you will need to keep coming back to this scale and to learn it thoroughly. Remember to use alternate picking – a common mistake is to use a downstroke when moving across to a higher string and an upstroke when coming the other way. Just start with a downstroke and alternate pick all the way across the guitar and back again.

■ THEORY

Usually, a scale begins and ends on the keynote (E in this case). However, it's normal practice on the guitar to play all the notes in a scale that you can reach from one position. This is why the scale begins on the low E and carries on across the guitar up to high G before turning round and heading all the way back.

PRO TIP

Scales needn't be boring. As we will see in the next few examples this scale can be very useful. But just to make it interesting, try experimenting with different rhythms and with grouping the notes together in different ways.

THE LOWER STRINGS

EXERCISE 31, **CD TRACK 23** / 'Double-Stop Blues'

Exercise 31 uses a series of riffs, based on the blues scale, that amount to a simple solo. The piece begins with four bars of rhythm guitar, during which there is a four-bar rest (silence) for you. Several consecutive empty bars or bar rests are often joined together, as seen here, with the number of bars written above. Count the beats in the empty bars as they go by to make sure you enter at the right time. All of the notes come from the blues scale except in bar 15, where we have a short chromatic run. The track was played using plenty of bite from the bridge pickup with a touch of added distortion. Alternate your pick strokes when playing the eighth-notes. Once again we have chord symbols that are based on the underlying harmony; in the next section we will be returning to this exercise in order to learn the rhythm guitar part.

■ THEORY

The lead guitar part in this example begins with two notes played at once. A two-note chord like this can be called a diad, which distinguishes it from a three-note chord, which is called a triad. It might just as commonly be called a 'double stop,' meaning simply 'two notes at once.'

PRO TIP

See if you can use the blues scale to make up some of your own riffs in the style of this piece.

Just to show you how versatile this scale can be, the next piece (Exercise 32) uses the blues scale but has nothing to do with blues. Played in a certain way, the blues scale contains some very dark sounds that are great for metal. For example, in the key of E, the B-flat – first fret on the A-string – is very effective.

We have a new type of note in this piece, the 16th-note.

There are four 16th-notes in one beat, and in bars six and eight you can see them beamed together four at a time. Since we count eighth-notes "one-and two-and" etc, we count 16th-notes "one-e-and-a two-e-and-a three-e-and-a four-e-and-a" and so on. This keeps the eighth-note count in the same place and just adds the two extra 16th-notes in each beat.

the electric guitar handbook

THE LOWER STRINGS

COUNTING 16TH-NOTES

As well as working out the letter names from the notation stave, you should have a close look at the tablature stave, as we are using both the open A-string and the fretted A at the fifth fret on the E-string. Using the fretted A allows us to use a new technique, which is called a pull-off. In the last beat of bar one, place your first and

EXERCISE 32, CD TRACK 24 / 'Midnight Metal'

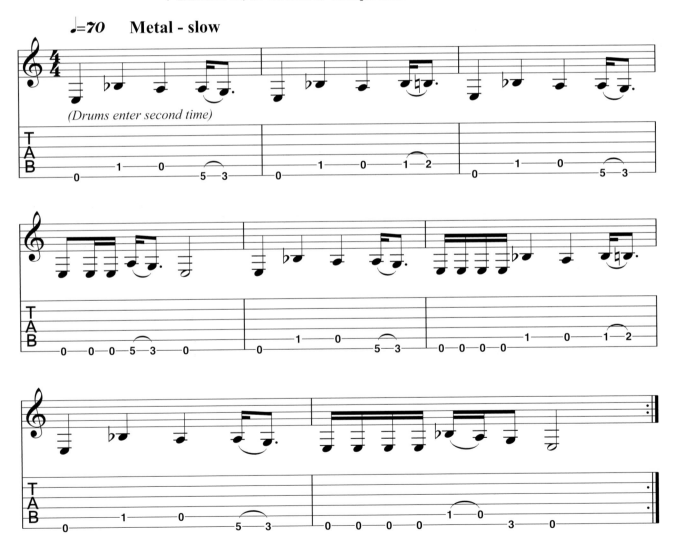

third fingers on the third and fifth frets of the low E-string. Play the note normally with the pick and then sound the G at the third fret by pulling your third finger off the string (in the direction of the A-string) with a plucking motion. Don't use your pick to play this note. In bars two and six we have the opposite motion, which is a 'hammer-on.' Place the first finger on the first fret of the A-string and pick the note, then hammer on with the second finger at the second fret.

PRO TIP

You will need to use a full-on distorted sound, but it's probably best to stick to your bridge pickup, as its natural brightness will help you to cut through the distortion.

■ THEORY

Pull-offs and hammer-ons are also sometimes known as 'slurs.' They are marked in the music by means of a curved line joining two notes of different pitch. A curved line joining two notes of the same pitch would be a tie – which, as we have seen, would create a longer note by adding the value of the second note to the first.

EXERCISE 33, CD TRACK 25 / Minor pentatonic scale in E

The blues scale is in fact a minor pentatonic scale with an added passing note. (B-flat in the key of E.) We will explain terms like major and minor in the future, but pentatonic is easy to explain; it means 'five note,' and there are many kinds of five-note scale, the minor being just one of them. I have included it here because some musicians like to use the minor pentatonic rather than the blues scale when making up riffs and solos. However, it is quite easy to convert a blues scale into a minor pentatonic by leaving out the added note. (Compare this scale to Exercise 30.) In future, as we learn more keys and scale shapes, we will stick to the blues scale and you can experiment with the minor pentatonic for yourself.

the electric guitar handbook

EXERCISE 34, CD TRACK 26 / C and G major pentatonic scales

Since we can have a minor pentatonic scale, it makes sense that we can also have a major pentatonic scale. On the CD track we have C major pentatonic followed immediately by G major pentatonic, both just as one-octave scales. This scale has a bright, twangy sound and is used in rock, blues, and country whenever the blues scale sounds too dark, sad, or just plain 'minor.' No fingering is given on either of these scales, but you should be able to work out a sensible fingering for your fret hand by now. Don't jump your hand up and down the guitar, stick to one finger for each fret.

EXERCISE 35, CD TRACK 27 / 'Country Cousin'

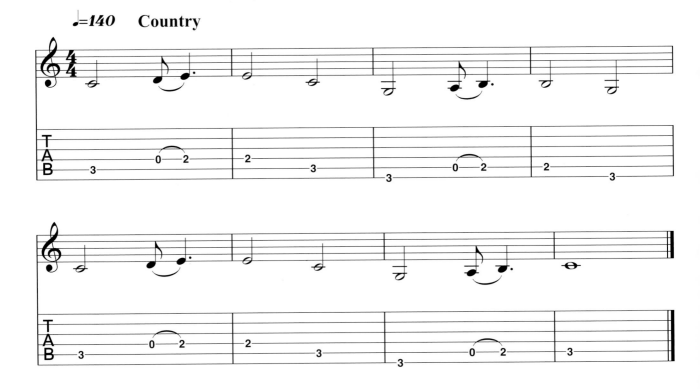

Staying with the lower end of the guitar, Exercise 35 uses the C major pentatonic and G major pentatonic scales to create a couple of riffs inspired by country and bluegrass. Playing on the lower frets adds to the twanginess, as do the hammer-ons, all of which start on an open string and should be done with your second finger. Stick to downstrokes with the pick for this one, and use your bridge pickup.

Exercise 36 demonstrates that you can add a passing note to the major pentatonic scale. This is a classic country lick often used at the end of a section of music or of a song. As in Exercise 35, the lick is played in both C and G.

EXERCISE 36, CD TRACK 28 / 'Finger-Licking Good'

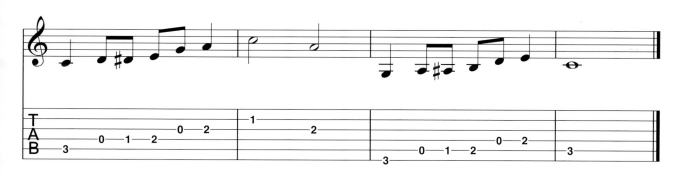

the electric guitar handbook

THE LOWER STRINGS

MAJOR SCALES AND KEYS

EXERCISE 37, CD TRACK 29 / C major scale

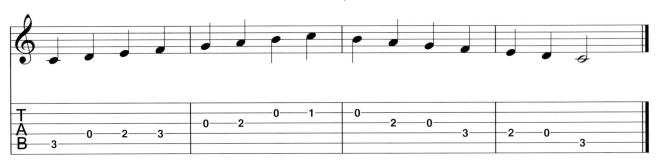

Moving on from pentatonic or five-note scales, we now have the major scale. The major scale is probably the most important scale in music. Not only do we derive many other scales from the major, it is also essential to the understanding of keys and chords. In this exercise we have a one-octave major scale played in the first position and using open strings whenever possible. The C major scale uses all the 'white notes.' There are no sharps or flats, and this gives it a structure that is common to all major scales, which is a sequence of whole steps (tones) and half-steps (semitones), as follows:

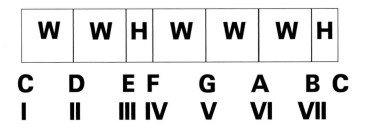

It's conventional to number the steps (or degrees) of a scale using Roman numerals.

If we were to repeat this pattern of whole step and half-step gaps starting on any other note we would also hear a major scale, but we would be in a different key. Here is G major for example:

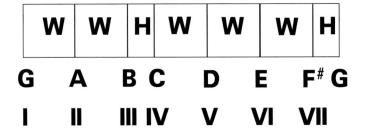

EXERCISE 38 / G major scale

Exercise 38 is the same information written out so it can be played on guitar. There is no CD track with this one – just play it by yourself.

Notice that to preserve the pattern of whole steps and half-steps we need to add F-sharp to produce a scale of G major. If we were to write a piece of music in the key of G we could put the F-sharp at the beginning of the piece as a key signature and it would save us having to write a sharp sign in front of every F in the piece. That's why there is an F-sharp in the key signature at the start of this example.

It's possible to start a major scale on every single letter name, including all of the sharp and flat notes. Each letter name or 'key' would have its own signature of sharps or flats at the beginning of the stave. Over the page is a chart that shows the key signatures and notes for all of the common keys.

Each letter name occurs once in each major scale. From this chart you can see that D major is D E F♯ G A B C♯ D. F Major is F G A B♭ C D E F. As an ongoing project, see if you can work out the rest of these scales for yourself. Then play each one on the guitar. If you are puzzled by E-sharp and C-flat, E-sharp is the same as F and C-flat is the same as B.

the electric guitar handbook

THE LOWER STRINGS

Key signatures and notes for all of the common keys

the electric guitar handbook

INTERVALS

Before we leave major scales, there is one more important concept that it is easy to demonstrate with a major scale. We have seen that it is normal to number the steps of the scale. There is a system in music that allows us to use numbers to describe the distance between any two notes; this is known as the interval. An interval is made up from two elements. Firstly a number describes how far it is from one note to the next. If C is the lowest note of an interval, the gap to D would be called a second, to E a third, to F a fourth and so on. It's quite easy to work out the number part of an interval – treat the lowest note as 'one' and then count up letter names until you arrive on the highest note. Here is an illustration showing all the intervals above C. Notice that you can carry on beyond the 'eighth,' or octave, to include ninths, tenths, and so on.

Simple intervals (intervals with one octave)

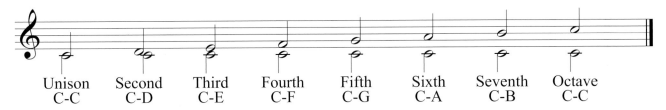

| Unison | Second | Third | Fourth | Fifth | Sixth | Seventh | Octave |
| C-C | C-D | C-E | C-F | C-G | C-A | C-B | C-C |

Compound intervals (intervals exceeding one octave)

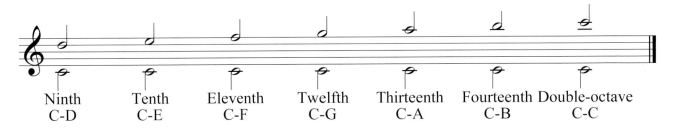

| Ninth | Tenth | Eleventh | Twelfth | Thirteenth | Fourteenth | Double-octave |
| C-D | C-E | C-F | C-G | C-A | C-B | C-C |

The second element in an interval is a word that describes its character. These words are major, minor, perfect, augmented and diminished. First we will learn how these intervals apply to a major scale:

Intervals in the major scale

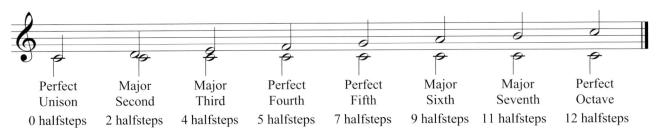

| Perfect Unison | Major Second | Major Third | Perfect Fourth | Perfect Fifth | Major Sixth | Major Seventh | Perfect Octave |
| 0 halfsteps | 2 halfsteps | 4 halfsteps | 5 halfsteps | 7 halfsteps | 9 halfsteps | 11 halfsteps | 12 halfsteps |

Here's a table which shows some other intervals that are not in the major scale:

Intervals outside the major scale

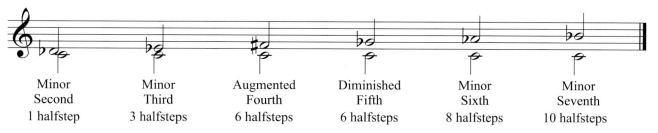

Minor Second	Minor Third	Augmented Fourth	Diminished Fifth	Minor Sixth	Minor Seventh
1 halfstep	3 halfsteps	6 halfsteps	6 halfsteps	8 halfsteps	10 halfsteps

The first table shows that all of the intervals in a major scale are either major or perfect. The second table shows the intervals made with notes that are not in the major scale. Notice that they are all minor, augmented, or diminished.

They say rules are made to be broken – but in the case of intervals, there are some rules that are never broken.

Fourths, fifths and octaves can only be perfect, augmented or diminished. They are never major or minor. Seconds, thirds, sixths, and sevenths are usually major or minor; they are never perfect.

Right now you probably feel like you've been in an algebra class. If you haven't fully grasped intervals, don't worry; at least you now know they exist and that they consist of a number and a word describing their character. Since a knowledge of intervals is important for understanding chords, we will explore them further when we come to Part Two.

Meanwhile the important thing to remember about intervals is that they describe the 'gap' between any two notes. Every melody, riff, or chord is made up of a series of intervals, and all the intervals sound different. With practice you can begin to tell them apart by ear, recognizing each interval's distinctive sound. This will make it possible to figure out for yourself what's happening on your favorite CD tracks.

In Section Four we will move on to blues-based rhythm playing. Here's a quick re-cap of the contents of Section Three: notes on the D, A, and E-strings; dotted notes and ties; accents and syncopation; letter names to the fifth fret and fifth-fret tuning; E blues scale and minor pentatonic; pull-offs and hammer-ons; C and G major pentatonic scales; major scales and key signatures; intervals.

rhythm guitar

Just in case you're feeling overloaded with theory, here's the perfect antidote – some blues rhythm guitar.

Here are two chord diagrams. We will be seeing more of these in the next chapter. They are not hard to understand. The O is an open string. The black blobs are where you put your finger or fingers, with the number telling you which finger to use. X tells you not to play the string – in this case we are only using the A and D strings for both of these two note chords (or diads). Beneath the diagram are the letter names of the notes that you are playing, together with numbers that describe the structure of the chord. With A5 we have just the root note A and the note five letter names up, E, so there is a 1 and a 5. In A6 we have the root note and the note six letter names up, F-sharp, so there is a 1 and a 6.

A5 and A6 chords

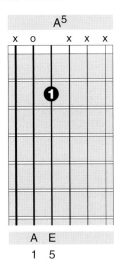
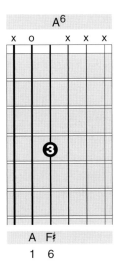

Give yourself a prize if you figured out that the interval for A5 is a perfect fifth, and that A6 is a major sixth. Sorry – intervals again!

Exercise 39 is the two chords played as a blues vamp; each chord is played twice in an eighth-note rhythm. Just play downstrokes.

Listen to CD Track 31 and check out the chunky rhythm sound. Exercise 40 uses a technique known as 'palm muting.' Rest the heel of your pick-hand on the lowest strings just in front of the bridge and play two notes with a downstroke. This muting

EXERCISE 39 CD TRACK 30 / Blues vamp on A

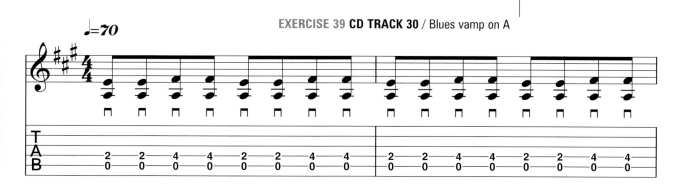

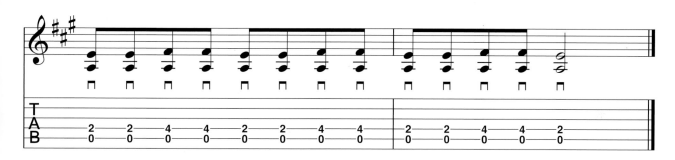

EXERCISE 40 CD TRACK 31 / Vamp with palm muting

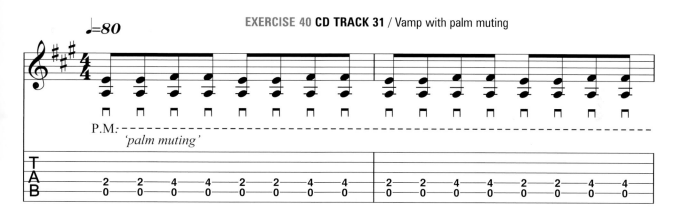

'palm muting'

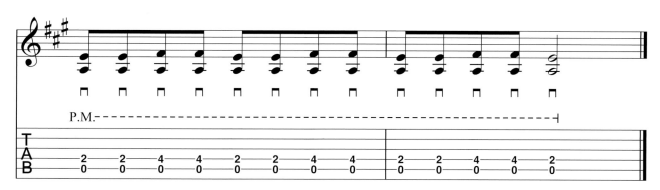

the electric guitar handbook

effect thickens the sound and is great for rhythm playing. You will need to experiment with the position of your hand when palm muting – the sound has more 'click' as you move away from the bridge and more 'thud' as you move nearer the bridge. Get too close to the bridge and you'll just get the normal guitar sound. You will be using just downstrokes the whole time.

■ THEORY

The palm muting is notated using the initials PM and a dotted line showing how long the muting lasts. Sometimes you will just need to mute one or two notes. Sometimes you will see the instruction "palm muting throughout" instead.

E5 and E6 chords

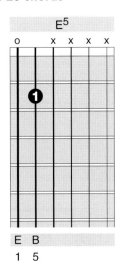 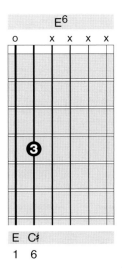

PRO TIP

Experiment with other ways of accenting this rhythm; for example, try only accenting beats two and four

The great thing about the A blues vamp is that you can pick it up and move across a string and you have an E blues vamp. Exercise 41 is four bars of E5 and E6, this time a little heavier, and with a distorted tone. Once again, it's all downstrokes, but notice that the downbeats are accented (played more strongly); this brings out the move from E5 to E6 more clearly.

Try your neck or middle pickup for a fat sound and add a touch of distortion or overdrive to warm things up a little.

■ THEORY

Underneath the tab stave in this example you can see the names of the chords we are playing, E5 and E6; this is the normal place to write chord symbols. Sometimes they are the actual chords you are playing (which they are here); sometimes they reflect the underlying harmony. It all depends on what the writer thinks you most need to know..

EXERCISE 41 **CD TRACK 32** / Blues vamp on E

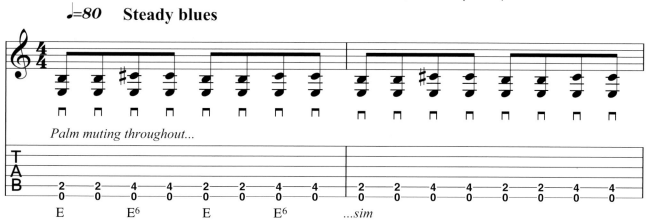

Palm muting throughout...

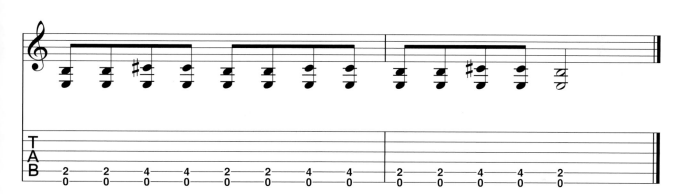

D5 and D6 chords

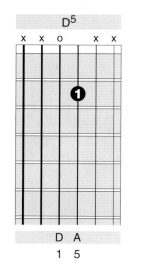

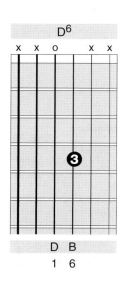

the electric guitar handbook

EXERCISE 42 **CD TRACK 33** / 12-bar blues in A

If we add the D5 and D6 vamp we have all we need to play a 12-bar blues. The 12-bar blues is so famous that bars and music stores are named after it. It is 12 bars long (of course) and follows a particular chord sequence. It can be played in any key, and uses chords I, IV, and V. (We say one, four, and five, but normally write them using Roman numerals the same as we do for steps of a scale.) If A is I, D is IV, and E is V.

Here is how the chords are laid out, one chord per bar:

I	I	I	I
IV	IV	I	I
V	IV	I	V

Or

A	A	A	A
D	D	A	A
E	D	A	E

On the CD it's palm-muted throughout and you should use only downstrokes for added emphasis.

■ THEORY

In a song, the 12-bar blues can be played again and again. Each time through is called a chorus. The blues vamp and the 12-bar blues are found throughout rock and blues music, from vintage solo blues artists like Robert Johnson ('Sweet Home Chicago') through rock'n'roll players like Chuck Berry ('Johnny B. Goode') to classic rock guys like Eric Clapton ('Crossroads'), and on to the present day.

B5 CHORD

Add the chord of B5 and you will have all you need to play the 12-bar blues in E. This is because in the key of E, E is chord I, and A is chord IV, so we only need B and we have chord V too.

E	E	E	E
A	A	E	E
B	A	E	B

For this example we are going to backtrack to Exercise 31, CD track 23. It starts off with the rhythm guitar playing alone through a four-bar intro, which gives us a chance to hear the groove clearly without the lead guitar part. The part alternates between the two-note E5 chord and the two-note E6 chord in a slightly different way to Exercise 41. We're only hitting both notes on the downbeats; on the upbeats just play the root

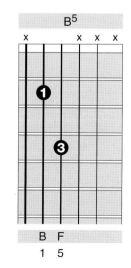

the electric guitar handbook

EXERCISE 43 CD TRACK 23 / 12-bar blues in E

♩=76 **Steady blues**

note of the chord. This gives the groove more of a bounce than playing both notes every time – check out the part on the CD. After four bars, the vamp is then taken round the standard 12-bar blues sequence, using the A5, A6, and B5 shapes once the lead guitar has joined in. There's no need for a B6 chord as we only stay on B for one bar – just playing B5 will sound fine. In the last three bars we break away from the vamp rhythm and play a single-note line that brings the blues to a strong conclusion.

If you check back to Exercise 31, you'll find you now have both guitar one and guitar two of this two-guitar piece. If you have a friend who can play guitar, try playing the piece together; take it in turns to play lead and rhythm, switching roles with each repeat. Try making up some of your own riffs using the blues scale and taking it in turns to solo.

SWING OR SHUFFLE

Up to now all of our eighth-notes have been what we call 'straight feel.' In other words, the time between all of the eighth-notes has been completely even. Now we are going to learn to shuffle. In the 'shuffle feel' the four main beats of the bar stay where they are, but the eighth-notes which fall in between are played later than usual, so that they seem to lean towards the next downbeat. What's really happening is that we are counting three eighth-notes to each beat, and then playing only on the first and third eighth-note. These three diagrams should make things clearer:

PRO TIP

It's important to be able to play in more than one key. Changing key from one song to the next makes the music more interesting for your audience; you also may need to change key to suit the pitch of your voice (or your singer's).

Straight feel

Clap	1 &	1 &	1 &	1 &
Tap	1	2	3	4

Triplets

Clap	123	123	123	123
Tap	1	2	3	4

Shuffle feel

Clap	1 3	1 3	1 3	1 3
Tap	1	2	3	4

the electric guitar handbook

EXERCISE 44 CD TRACK 34 / 12-bar shuffle in A

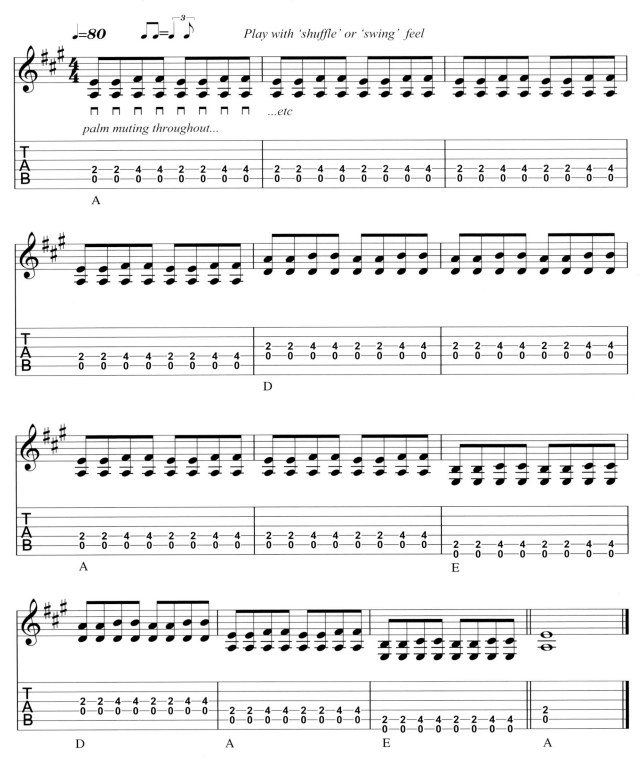

Play with 'shuffle' or 'swing' feel

...etc

palm muting throughout...

■ THEORY

Sometimes we play three notes in the time of two, such as three eighth-notes in one quarter-note beat. These 'three to a beat' eighth-notes are called 'triplets' and usually beamed together like this:

Many modern editions leave out the small 3 because it's usually easy to tell when the music is in triplets. Any type of note can be a triplet. You could have three quarter-notes in the time of one half-note. Or even three half-notes in the time of a whole-note.

When it comes to writing music with shuffle feel (also known as swing feel) it actually looks the same as straight feel. At the beginning of the piece, it will say 'shuffle' or 'swing' or will have a sign that looks like this:

Exercise 44 is a 12-bar blues just like Exercise 42, but this time with a shuffle feel. Have a listen to the CD track and you will probably realise that you've heard this rhythmic effect before, as it is very common in jazz and blues.

Now that you have mastered the swing feel, we are going to switch to the key of E. Exercise 45 is a blues that begins with one chorus of blues vamp and then adds two more choruses of single-note riffs based on the blues scale that we learned in Section Two. Notice the sign at the beginning that tells you that a pair of quavers is to be played as the first and third note of a triplet – in other words, swing!

Chorus two keeps to the low notes of the blues scale. Pick with downstrokes on the downbeats and upstrokes on the up beats. The first bar is given for you.

For the third and final chorus we are using the higher notes of the blues scale beginning with some double stops – two notes played at the same time.

We are almost at the end of Part One. We've covered a huge amount of ground, and you should be beginning to feel confident, not only that you can play the guitar but also that you understand what's going on in the music. We've covered technical aspects of using the pick and fret hand, all of the notes up to the fifth fret of the guitar, reading music and tablature, and also looked at various scales and aspects of music theory.

PRO TIP
Steal some of these riffs to make up your own solo!

EXERCISE 45 CD TRACK 35 / E blues rhythm

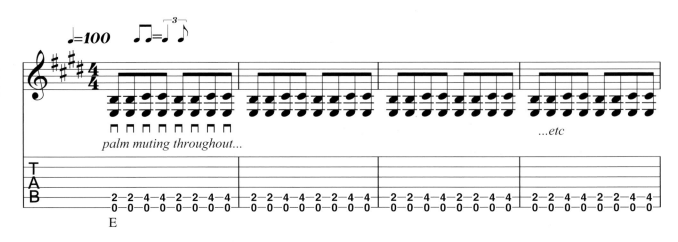

palm muting throughout...

...etc

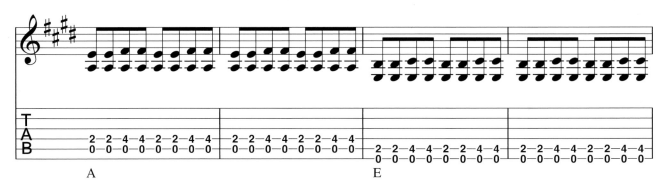

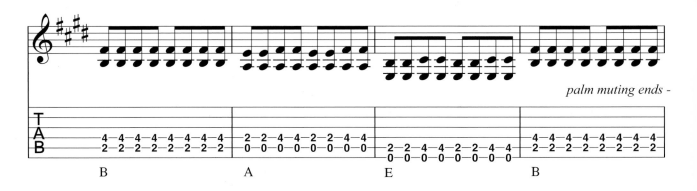

palm muting ends -

EXERCISE 45 CD TRACK 35 / E blues solo one

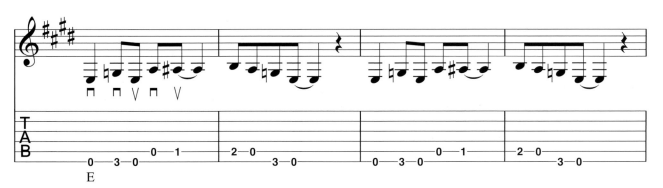

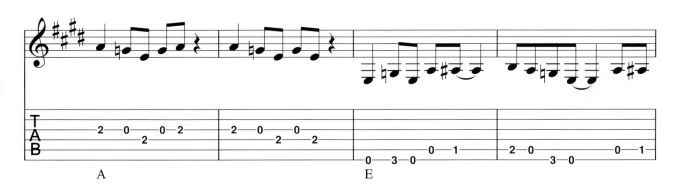

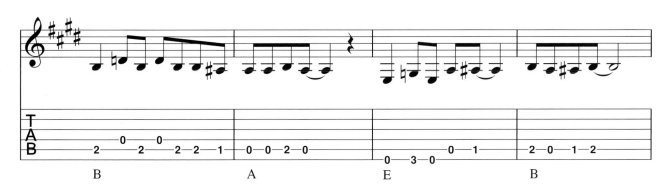

the electric guitar handbook

EXERCISE 45 CD TRACK 35 / E blues solo two

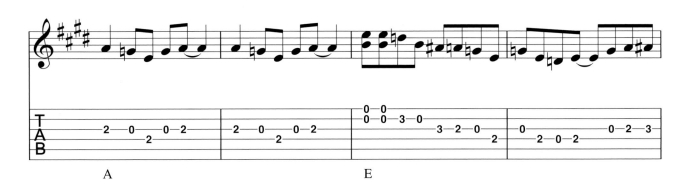

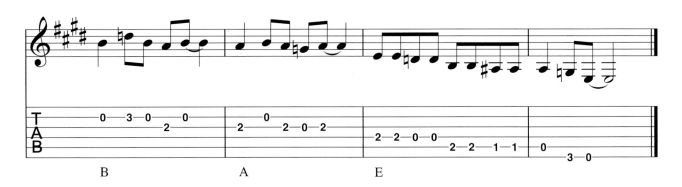

PRO TIP

See if you can sing the next note before you go looking for it on the guitar; this helps to fix its pitch clearly in your brain.

the electric guitar handbook

I would like to end this chapter by introducing the idea of playing by ear. I have chosen three well-known tunes for you to play, but have only written out the first few bars. I know they're not very rock'n'roll, but for this exercise they need to be tunes that everyone knows. These melodies are not on the CD; you have to read the notes that are given and finish each melody by hearing the tune in your head and finding the notes on the guitar. When you've done these, think of other tunes that you know and see if you can figure those out on the guitar too. Or listen to your favorite CD and see if you can work out some of the guitar riffs.

EXERCISE 46 / 'Twinkle Twinkle Little Star'

continue...

EXERCISE 47 / 'My Country 'Tis Of Thee' / 'God Save The Queen'

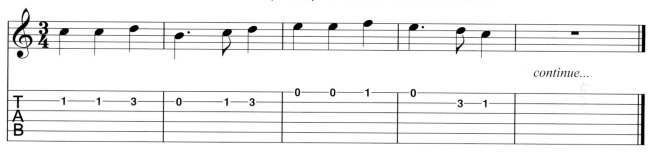

continue...

EXERCISE 48 / 'Yankee Doodle'

continue...

the electric guitar handbook

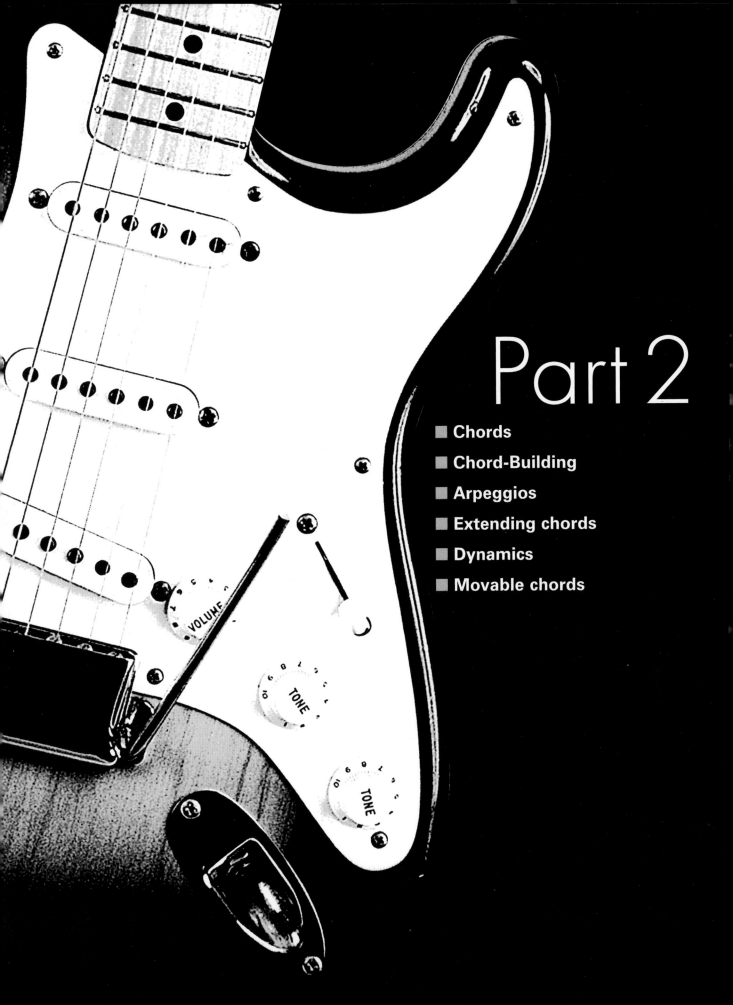

Part 2

- Chords
- Chord-Building
- Arpeggios
- Extending chords
- Dynamics
- Movable chords

chords

We saw chord diagrams for two-note chords in the previous section. In this section we will look at chords with four, five, and six notes.

Start by holding down this E major shape and playing a downstroke on each string in turn, listening to make sure that all six notes are sounding and that you are not accidentally silencing an open string with the underside of one of your fret hand fingers.

PRO TIP

Using your fingers on their tips is particularly important when it comes to playing chords.

Now have a listen to CD track 36. You will hear the E major chord (right) played just once, then twice, then four times, and finally eight times in a bar. Grab your guitar, hold

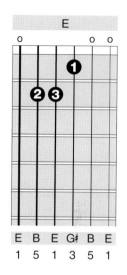

EXERCISE 49, **CD TRACK 36** / E major chord

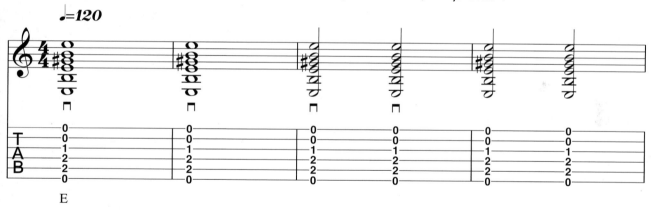

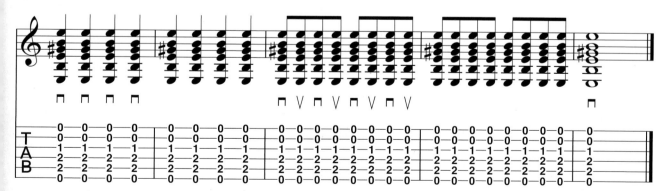

down the chord and play along. Use downstrokes until you get to bars seven and eight, where you should start using alternate down and up strokes on the eighth-notes. It is written on the part for you. Ensure you hit all six strings with every stroke.

■ **THEORY**

This method of playing chords is known as 'strumming.'

Open-string chords

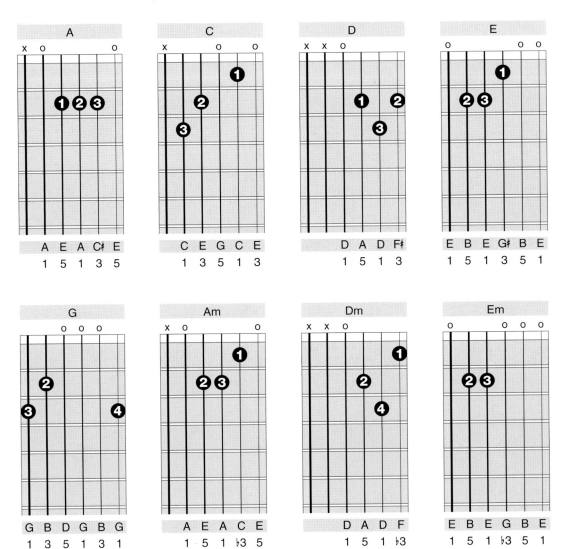

Exercise 49 should have loosened up your strumming hand, so now let's learn some more chords. Sometimes these diagrams are referred to as 'chord shapes,' and these particular chord shapes are known as 'open string chords' as they all involve open strings as well as fretted notes. As they are the simplest and most basic chords in guitar music you should learn them thoroughly – don't forget to learn each one's

EXERCISE 50, CD TRACK 37 / More chords

name, too. Many of the coming exercises will use one or more of these shapes so it might be a good idea to bookmark this page. Listen to CD track 37 and you will hear how each of these chords should sound. Each one begins with a downstroke and is then played as an arpeggio – one note at a time.

■ THEORY

When we speak about a major chord we usually just say its letter name, so D major would be called just D. With minor chords we always use the full name, A minor or D minor. When writing minor chords it's normal to use the abbreviation 'm,' as in Am for A minor or Dm for D minor.

the electric guitar handbook

EXERCISE 51, **CD TRACK 38** / Majors moving

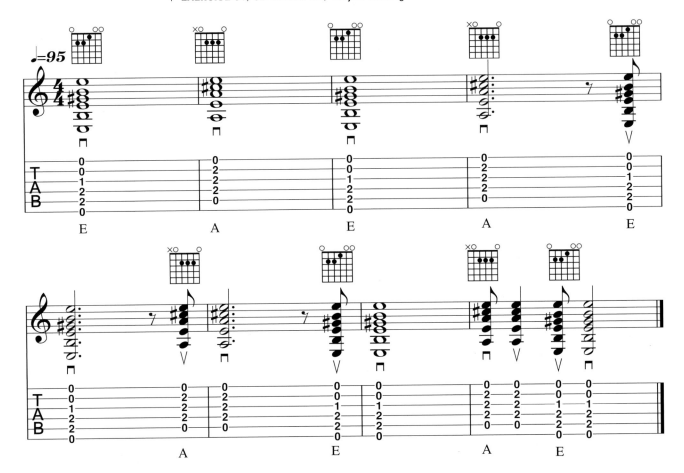

Exercise 51 is all about shifting between two chord shapes. It's one thing to be able to hold a chord down, but can you move to another one and arrive at the right time? E and A are not too hard to hold down, and the trick to moving between them is to keep your fingers close to the guitar and move each finger as smoothly and directly as possible to where it's meant to be going. This may seem obvious, but you'd be surprised how often a beginner rips all three fingers way off the guitar and tries to slam them down on the next chord. Practice more slowly than the CD track if you have to, and go for accuracy rather than speed. We start with downstrokes, but after the first four bars we add an upstroke before each downstroke chord. The last bar has a quicker change – you'll get it with some practice!

■ THEORY

Above the music stave in this exercise there are miniature chord diagrams or 'chord grids' as they are sometimes called. Not all guitar music has these; sometimes you just get the shapes at the beginning of the piece and sometimes you're left to figure out the shapes for yourself. In this book you'll always know what shapes to use, but there won't always be these mini-grids.

PRO TIP

For this track use the bridge pickup on your guitar and crank the gain on your amp to the point where you're just on the edge of distortion. Most amps have a master volume which you turn down to control the overall output. Keep the treble control low so the sound is fat and warm rather than bright and crunchy. There are just guitar and drums on this track; this kind of stripped-down rock is inspired by bands like The White Stripes.

the electric guitar handbook

EXERCISE 52, **CD TRACK 39** / 'Joe Strumming'

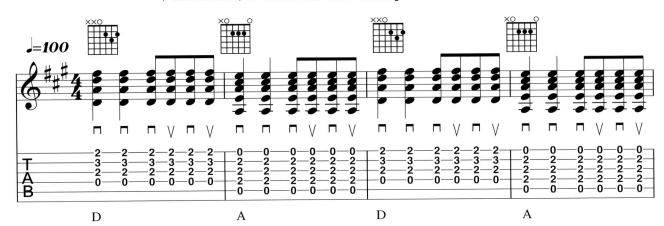

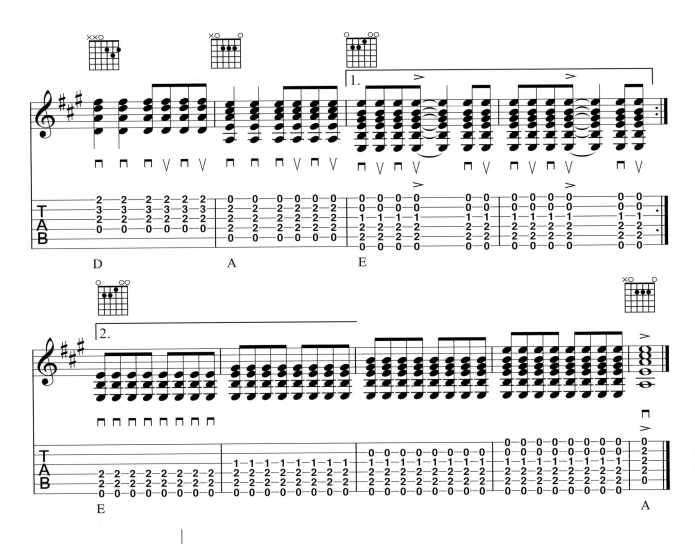

Strumming is usually made up of a mixture of downstrokes and upstrokes, as you'll find in Exercise 52. We're also adding the D major chord to the mix and introducing accents. This is the accent symbol:

>

It tells you to play a single note or chord louder than those surrounding it – it's a way of emphasizing the rhythm at that point. Check out the CD track to hear the accents on the E chord in this example. Be careful not to mix up the accent sign with the upstroke sign:

V

 THEORY

Did you notice the three sharps at the beginning of the stave? We are in the key of A major. We also have a 'first time' bar with a repeat, and a 'second time' bar leading to a gradual build up on an E chord before we arrive home, or 'resolve' on to the key chord of A major.

the electric guitar handbook

EXERCISE 53, **CD TRACK 40** / 'Slight Return'

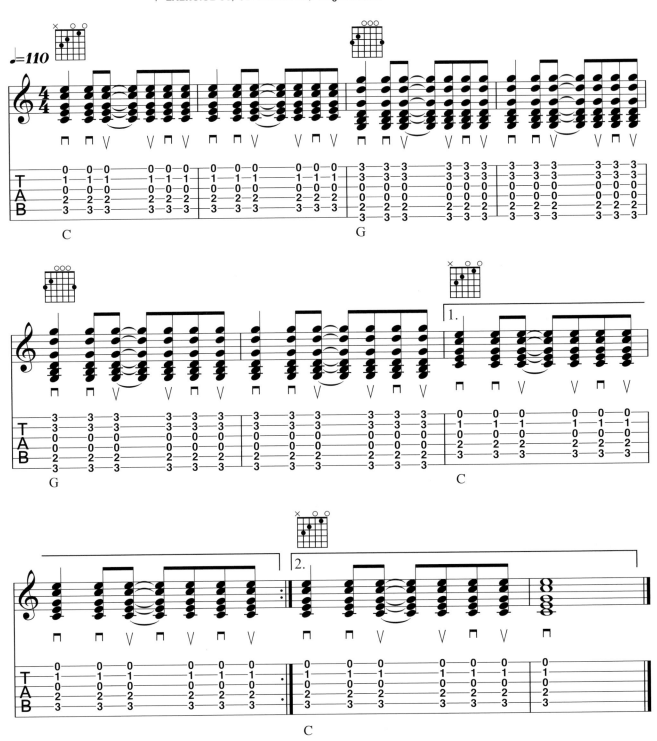

Exercise 53 introduces some syncopated strumming (where the accents fall on weak beats) by using tied notes in the middle of the bar. We're also using two more major chords: C and G. If you head back to CD Track 7 you can hear this rhythm guitar part in context. The chords are simple but you'll need to follow the pick directions closely to get the feel right. As with picking single notes, there is an underlying principle here – the downbeats are all downstrokes and the upbeats are all upstrokes. Your pick hand moves smoothly to and fro across the guitar striking the strings only when needed. Track 7 was mixed with the lead guitar part nice and loud so you'll need to listen carefully to hear what's happening in that rhythm part; CD track 40 is the rhythm part soloed so you can really focus on that 'one two-and (three) -and four-and' rhythm. This time the music is written out with a repeat sign and a first and second time bar.

PRO TIP

C and G are very common keys for guitar music, so being able to shift between these two chord shapes is important. Use fingers two, three, and four for the G chord – it will be easier in the long run. Practice moving the fret hand fingers to their destination by the shortest route. If you practice slowly (which you should), always imagine an underlying beat so that you practice playing in time.

EXERCISE 54, CD TRACK 41 / 'Minor Mishap'

There's something bright and solid about a major chord, whereas there's something dark and sad about a minor chord. 'Minor Mishap' takes a look at the three open-string minor chords we are learning: Am, Dm, and Em. We're in twangy surf-guitar territory here, and each chord is followed by an arpeggio-based melody. Watch out for the sudden appearance of the E major chord in bar 13. Notice the wiggly line with an arrow before each chord. That tells you to make a slow downstroke, playing the notes one at a time as a 'spread' chord. The odd one out is in bar five, where the arrow points in the other direction and tells you to do an upstroke. These 'spread' chords are also 'arpeggios,' although here we are closer to the original meaning of the word, which is 'harp-like.' If you have a delay pedal, experiment with a rhythmic delay effect like you can hear on the CD.

PRO TIP

Be careful to avoid the open E-string (sixth string) when you're playing D minor or D major, as it does not belong. You can get away with the open A-string as it does belong in the chord, but chords tend to sound best with the root note (the note that gives the chord its name) in the bass.

■ **THEORY**

A chord played with the root note in the bass is known as a chord in 'root position.'

the electric guitar handbook

CHORD-BUILDING ONE

What makes a chord? Technically, a chord is a group of notes played at the same time. Yes, any notes. However, the chords that we use in the sort of music that you hear every day (excluding music that belongs to the avant-garde or contemporary classical tradition) follow a structure that has been established for several hundred years. The most basic chord is a triad. A triad consists of a root, a third, and a fifth, and there are only four kinds of triads:

A major triad consists of a root, major third and perfect fifth. C major = C E G
A minor triad consists of a root, minor third and perfect fifth. C minor = C E♭ G
A diminished triad consists of a root, minor third and diminished fifth. C diminished = C E♭ G♭
An augmented triad consists of a root, major third and augmented fifth. C augmented = C E G♯

Of these four types of triad, major and minor chords are the most common. The next question is, 'What has all this to do with the chords that we are playing?' Take a look at the chord diagram for C major. Look at the letter names that you are playing in this chord – they're written underneath the diagram. You will find that all the notes are either C, E, or G. That's root, third, or fifth. In fact, if you look at any of the major chords that we have learned so far, you will see that each chord contains just three different notes, and that they are always the root, major third and perfect fifth. All the minor chords we've learned have a root, minor third and perfect fifth.

Notes for the common major chords.

MAJOR CHORDS

Chord	Root	Third	Fifth
C	C	E	G
D♭	D♭	F	A♭
D	D	F♯	A
E♭	E♭	G	B♭
E	E	G♯	B
F	F	A	C
F♯	F♯	A♯	C♯
G♭	G♭	B♭	D♭
G	G	B	D
A♭	A♭	C	E♭
A	A	C♯	E
B♭	B♭	D	F
B	B	D♯	F♯

If you wanted to turn a minor chord into a major chord, just raise the third one half-step or semitone (that's the same as one fret). Look at your chord shapes again and check out the difference between D minor and D major, or A minor and A major or E minor and E major. You'll find only one note is different, it's always the third, and it's one fret higher in pitch.

Augmented and diminished chords are much less common, but you can build them by changing the notes in major or minor chords as follows.

To build an augmented chord, take the notes of the major chord and sharpen the fifth.

To build a diminished chord, take the notes of the minor chord and flatten the fifth.

As guitarists, we can put this knowledge about triads to good use. At the moment, a C major chord is a shape on the guitar. However, anywhere that we play the notes C, E and G would be a C major chord. We can choose to play these notes low or high, tightly clustered or widely spread out. We can play just three notes, or double the notes in the chord to create a thicker texture. There are literally hundreds of possibilities with just this one chord of three notes.

Every guitarist begins by learning chord shapes; a little knowledge of chord building allows us to move on to choosing the sounds we want to make by knowing what notes to play, rather than being limited by the few shapes we know.

We will return to triads and chord building in the next section.

Notes for the common minor chords.

MINOR CHORDS

Chord	Root	Third	Fifth
C	C	Eb	G
C#	C#	E	G#
D	D	F	A
D#	D#	F#	A#
Eb	Eb	Gb	Bb
E	E	G	B
F	F	Ab	C
F#	F#	A	C#
G	G	Bb	D
G#	G#	B	D#
Ab	Ab	Cb	Eb
A	A	C	E
Bb	Bb	Db	F
B	B	D	F#

the electric guitar handbook

EXERCISE 55, CD TRACK 42 / 'Big Chords One'

As your guitar playing improves you can develop an appreciation of different styles of music and how different bands get their sound. Exercise 55 uses the major chords we have learned so far, plus the new chord of Dsus4 (right), to explore some indie rock jangle.

In a sus4 chord the third of the major chord is raised (suspended) one fret. Compare this shape to the regular D chord and you'll see there's a higher note on the first string, G instead of F-sharp. We begin by strumming the major chords (this piece uses all five open string shapes), keeping to the first beat of the bar and letting the notes ring on. As the music builds, the strumming gets busier and looser, but you should stick mostly to downstrokes for this piece. Play along with the CD and listen closely to be sure that your timing doesn't drift out. It may seem obvious, but to play in a band with other musicians we need to learn to listen to each other, and when you're trying to get your fingers round the chords and rhythms that can be difficult. So learn your part thoroughly and aim to keep your ears open while you're playing.

When we reach the Dsus4 chord we repeat the chord sequence, four times through altogether. We'll add a lead guitar part to this piece in the next section.

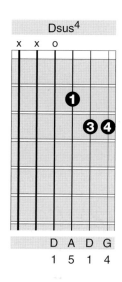

Dsus^4

D A D G
1 5 1 4

PRO TIP

Simple, heavy rhythmic parts like this are best played using just downstrokes. As we know, alternate downstrokes and upstrokes are more common.

■ THEORY

'Sus' is short for suspended. There are two common types of suspended chord, the sus2 and the sus4. In these chords the major third is altered, either by raising it up a half-step/semitone so that it becomes the fourth, or lowering it a whole step so that it becomes the second. Suspended chords have a restless quality that suits many different kinds of music, but they are particularly popular with guitarists in jangly rock or indie bands.

Up to now we've been strumming away on six, five, or four strings depending on which chord we're playing. Very often guitar players move the strumming around, sometimes hitting the bass strings, sometimes the higher strings. 'Low Strum, High Strum' demonstrates this technique in the style of a slow rock ballad. It also gives us a chance to start mixing up some of the major and minor shapes we've learned. There are no chord grids on this one – use the open string chord shapes from Exercise 51. You'll need to memorize those shapes – and Dsus4, which first appeared in Exercise 55 above.

The strumming is mostly in eighth-notes, with a tie between the fourth and fifth eighth-note in each bar. This is a common rock rhythm that you'll recognise from many songs you've heard. Pick directions are included for the first few bars, and sometimes the strum moves into sixteenth-notes to fill out a beat or two. There's just guitar and drums on the CD track, so you can hear what the guitar is doing and copy what you hear. For the most part, the low notes of the chord are sounded at the start of the bar, with the higher notes filling in the rhythm in the rest of the bar. Follow the tab or notation and you should get the feel for it.

If you find the chord changes difficult, you could break the piece into easier steps. To begin with, work on the strumming on just one chord, over and over, until you have the feel right. Next, practice going through the chord changes playing each new chord on only the first beat of the bar. Then, try the changes and the strumming together, slowly. Eventually you'll be able to play the piece at full speed.

PRO TIP

The end of bar eight has a row of XXX notes; these are open strings muted with the left hand. It's not unusual sometimes to strike the open strings between chord changes. They can be muted or otherwise, but be careful not to overdo it.

CHORDS

EXERCISE 56, **CD TRACK 43** / 'Low Strum, High Strum'

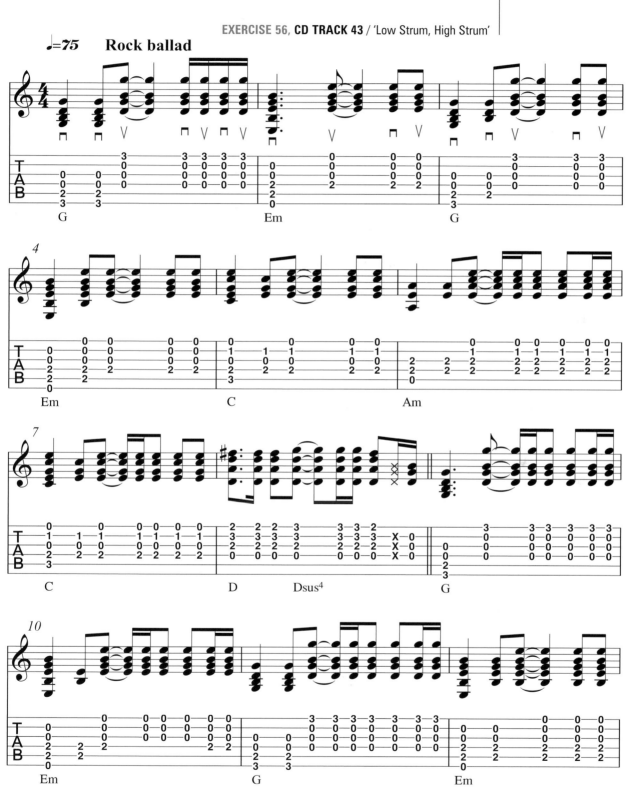

continued over page

the electric guitar handbook

EXERCISE 56 *continued*

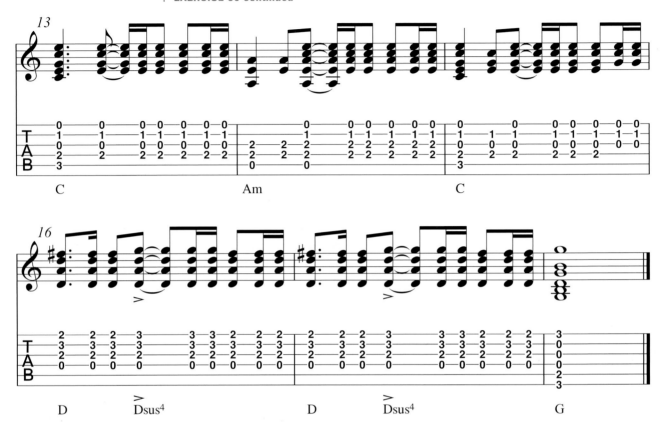

Exercise 57 uses the same chord sequence as Exercise 56 but this time instead of the low notes/high notes approach we begin each bar with just the root note of the chord. The root note played on its own in this way makes an effective bassline, and mimics the effect of two instruments playing together. As we repeat the chord sequence, the bassline is now fleshed out with the addition of 'passing notes' between the main root notes; these passing notes are also sometimes called 'connecting notes' – it's easy to see why. Follow the pick directions carefully, and balance the volume of your bassline with the volume of your strummed chords.

PRO TIP
Listen closely to the CD track. You'll hear that sometimes the strumming is heavier or lighter and that the bassline is mostly played strongly. Bringing this sort of light and shade to your playing will make you a more interesting player.

the electric guitar handbook

EXERCISE 57, CD TRACK 44 / 'Low Strum, High Strum' (with bassline)

continued over page

the electric guitar handbook

EXERCISE 57 *continued*

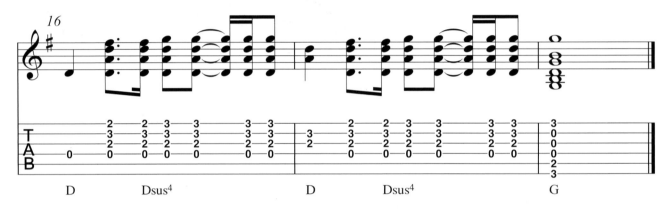

Exercise 58, 'Big Chords Two,' takes the same approach as Exercise 57 but adds a level of difficulty, with a faster and more complex bassline. From bar nine onwards we abandon the bassline and instead take up some heavy strumming, keeping to the lower notes of the chord. Notice that the music gets steadily louder during this section; we call this a crescendo, which is often shortened to 'cresc…' in the music. A crescendo can also be shown using this sign, which musicians often call a hairpin:

We will return to this exercise in the next section to add a lead guitar part.

■ THEORY

The opposite of a crescendo is a decrescendo or a diminuendo. Diminuendo is often shortened to 'dim…' We can also use this hairpin sign if we wish to notate a decrease in volume level:

PRO TIP

For added power, try sticking to downstrokes when you come to bar nine; gradually dig in harder with the pick to create the crescendo.

the electric guitar handbook

EXERCISE 58, CD TRACK 45 / 'Big Chords Two'

A simple bassline that will fit under any chord can be made from just the root and the fifth of the chord. This is very common in folk and country styles. The root is played on the first beat of the bar, with the fifth on the third beat of the bar. Beats two and four are then filled by strumming the higher notes of the chord. Exercise 59 demonstrates the technique using just C and G chords; you should try the same approach with the other chords that you know, working out where the root and fifth are for each shape.

The second half of the piece, from bar eight onwards, introduces basslines connecting the roots. We are in the key of C major, and all these notes come from the C major scale. If you like this style, experiment with any songs you know, and see if you can fit in connecting basslines in the same way.

PRO TIP

When you play a C major chord your third finger is on the root note, C. The best way to play the fifth, G, on the lowest string is just to 'hop' your third finger across, hopping back again to C when you need it.

■ **THEORY**

Can you work out which note of a chord is the root and which is the fifth? The root should be simple; it's the name note of the chord. To find the fifth, count five letter names up the major scale, starting with the root as 'one.'

For example:

1	2	3	4	5
C	D	E	F	G

1	2	3	4	5
G	A	B	C	D

Below the chord diagrams in this book you will find numbers that you can also use to find the root (1) or the fifth (5).

EXERCISE 59, CD TRACK 46 / G and C root and fifth

Back in Part One, in Exercise 35, we learnt a cool country-style hammer-on lick. In Exercise 60 we use this lick as a bassline, adding strummed chords above in true flat-picking country style. The bassline is played entirely with downstrokes, and each bass note and hammer-on is followed by the top three notes of the chord played with a down and upstroke. Hold down the C or G chord shape throughout. It's a tricky piece and requires very accurate picking; play the bassline strongly and the chords lightly. You will probably need to work slowly at first.

This style of playing goes back to the early days of country with tracks by The Carter Family and others; it also the mainstay of bluegrass rhythm guitar. If these styles aren't your thing, learn it anyway and see if you can apply it your own kind of music; you may come up with a whole new style of your own.

PRO TIP
When you've mastered this track, try playing it without looking at your hands.

EXERCISE 60, **CD TRACK 47** / 'Twang Thang'

CHORD-BUILDING TWO: SEVENTH CHORDS

We build chords in thirds; each time we go from root to third, or third to fifth, we are going up three notes. If we carry on adding notes to a chord in the same way, the next note would be the seventh. There are two kinds of seventh, major seventh and minor seventh. For example, C to B would be a major seventh, whereas C to B-flat would be a minor seventh. One way of making it easier to recognize what kind of seventh you have is to compare it to the octave. C to B, a major seventh, is one half-step or semitone away from being a full octave; C to B-flat, a minor seventh, is a whole step away from being a full octave.

You can add a major or minor seventh to any triad, and end up with some great sounding – and some weird sounding – chords. Let's look at what kind of chord you get when you add a minor seventh to a major triad.

Here are eight new chord diagrams, most of which are based on the open string major chords that we learned back in Exercise 50.

Our E major chord has become E7; there are two versions of this chord because it is possible to add the note D to an E major chord in two ways.

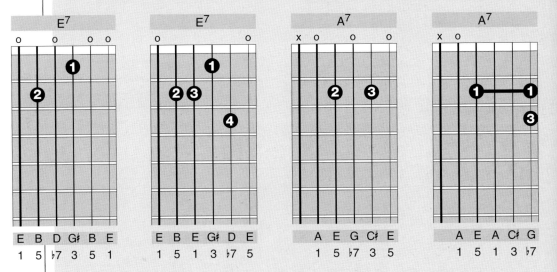

E⁷	E⁷	A⁷	A⁷

Seventh chords sound great in the blues and related styles. In fact, they sound better than major chords, and most blues guitarists would instinctively use sevenths in preference to the plain major chord. Exercise 61, 'Drive-in Groove,' takes a two-chord groove (G7 and C7) in a 1960s rhythm & blues style and adds a turnaround on A7 and D7; play it twice and then take the two-bar ending. There's also a cool single-note riff

There are also two versions of A7, in which we add the note G to the A major chord.

To make C7, we have added the note B-flat to C major.

To make D7, we have added the note C to D major.

To make G7, we have added the note F to G major.

B7 is a new chord that we have not seen before, but it consists of the notes of B major (B, D-sharp, and F-sharp) with the added note A.

Get used to calling these chords by name. For A7 we say 'A seven'; E7 is 'E seven'; and so on. For reasons that will be explained later these 'major triad with minor seventh' chords are also sometimes known as 'dominant sevenths.'

We will return to chord building soon, but first some music that actually uses our new chord shapes.

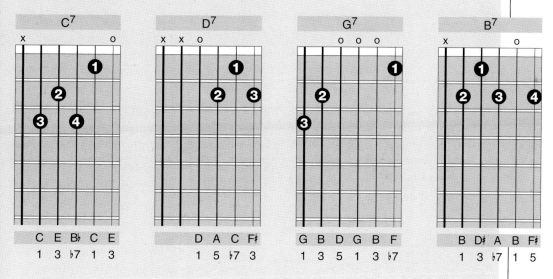

linking the chords and kicking the piece off; great for practicing going from single notes to strumming. Some strums are in brackets, which is a way of showing a de-accented chord or note, one which is strummed lighter than the others or perhaps not really meant to be there at all. This track was played using a clean, bright sound and the middle pickup of a Strat.

EXERCISE 61, **CD TRACK 48** / 'Drive-in Groove'

♩=100 **Rhythm and blues**

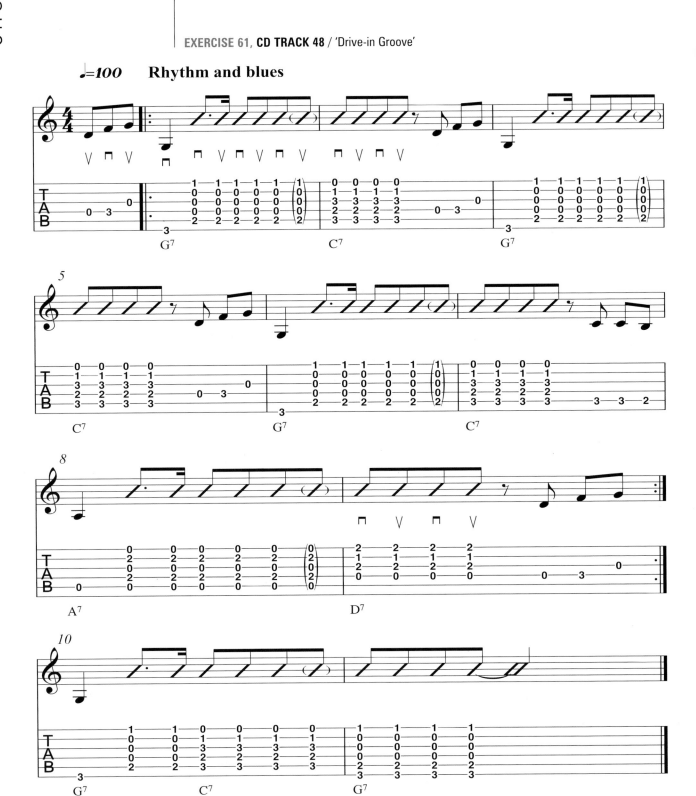

■ THEORY

Notice that the strumming is notated differently this time; the notation stave uses 'stem' notes and just gives you the strumming rhythm together with the single notes; the tab stave spells out which notes to play. You could easily see these different methods swapped around in other music books, depending on what the writer thought you most needed.

PRO TIP

By now, you should be used to counting eighth notes: 'one-and two-and three-and four-and.' Sixteenth notes can be trickier. The best way is 'one-e-and-a two-e-and-a three-e-and-a four-e-and-a.' For example, on the second beat of bar two, play a downstroke as you say 'two,' keep your hand moving as you say 'e' and 'and' and then play an upstroke as you say 'a.' Listen to the track and copy what you hear.

Here are the counts for different 16th-note patterns.

To round off this first section of Part Two we are going to learn the rhythm part to CD Track 15, 'Shadow Walk.' The lead guitar part can be found at Exercise 19. This track uses all the major open-string chords we have learned, most of the minor chords, and E7 and B7 chords as well. There are also several different kinds of strumming, from chords that are spread and held at the beginning, to accented downbeats in bar eight and a more filled-out strum in bars nine to 16.

There's a stereo echo effect on the track; the rhythm guitar is panned slightly to the left of the stereo image, but the echo effect is panned to the right, adding a mysterious quality as the sound spreads across.

PRO TIP

When playing B7 use the tip of finger two to mute the low E string. We don't want that note to sound and muting it allows you to be more relaxed with the strumming and not worry about accidentally touching that string with the pick.

the electric guitar handbook

■ THEORY

Notice the hairpin in bar 15; this means you should get louder by digging in harder with the pick when you strum that bar.

EXERCISE 62, CD TRACK 15 / 'Shadow Walk' rhythm part

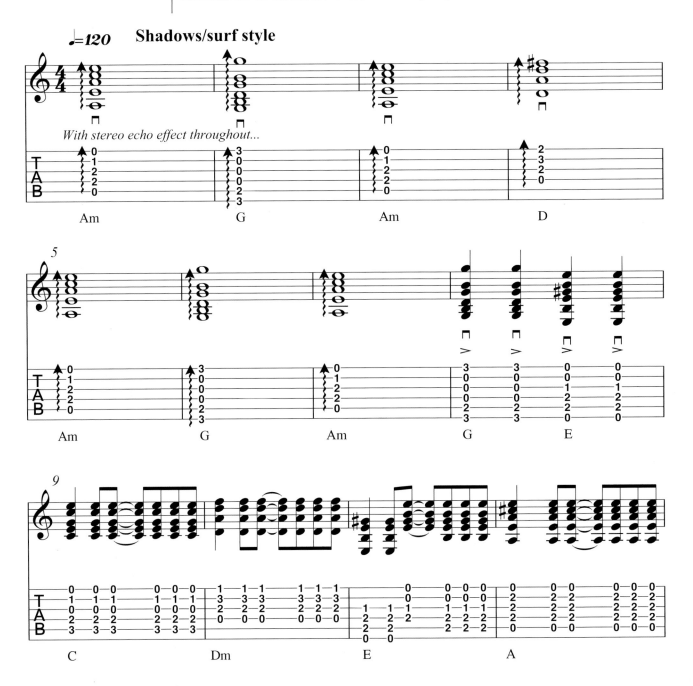

With stereo echo effect throughout...

the electric guitar handbook

In this section we have learned the basic major, minor and seventh chord shapes and how to move between them. We have introduced arpeggios and looked at simple and more complex strumming, and have also experimented with adding basslines and passing notes. In the next section we will return to arpeggios, and look at ways of using the chords of a song to create a second guitar part. There will also be some new techniques and more complex strumming.

chords and arpeggios

We know that an arpeggio is a chord played one note at a time. Very often the lead guitar parts that we hear filling in the background on recordings use arpeggios. In this example we have the rhythm part from Exercise 55 (CD track 42) combined with an arpeggio-style lead guitar part. There is also one new technique: the slide. A slide is notated with a straight line connecting two notes:

PRO TIP

Two or three string arpeggios like these are best played using strict 'alternate picking' – that means down, up, down, up and so on. You could also try 'fingerstyle' – using your picking-hand thumb on the lowest note and index and middle fingers on the others. There is also a third style, using pick and fingers; sometimes this is called 'hybrid' picking. Use the pick on the lowest note, and your middle and third fingers to play the others. Experiment and see if these styles suit you.

Play the first note as usual, then, maintaining finger pressure, slide up the string to the fret indicated. Check out bars four and eight, and listen to the track to hear how it is done.

This lead guitar part begins with arpeggios on the middle three strings before switching to the top three strings. The jump in pitch adds to the build-up as the strumming in the rhythm guitar part gets busier.

Notice the 'let ring' instruction at the beginning – when playing arpeggios we very often let the notes overlap as much as possible. Mostly these arpeggio notes are found in the chord shapes that the rhythm guitar is playing, except in bars four and eight where we slide up to the fourth fret under the Dsus4 chord. Once we've crossed over to the top three strings the top E string acts as a drone, ringing on over the G chord even though it doesn't really belong. When you're playing arpeggios you can experiment by adding notes that aren't in the original chords – you can discover some really interesting sounds.

EXERCISE 63, **CD TRACK 49** / 'Big Chords One' lead part

DOUBLE TRACKING

Playing music together with other musicians is very rewarding and great fun – certainly more fun than practicing on your own. As this book progresses you'll find many pieces that are arranged for two guitars, so I hope you'll be able to try them out with your guitar-playing friends.

In fact you could play any of these pieces on two guitars – two guitars playing exactly the same music, tightly synchronized, can sound very good – it's what we call 'double tracking' and is often used to add 'fatness' to guitar parts. It works particularly well if the two guitars make a different sound; one thick and fat, one bright and trebly. On recordings the two parts can be panned to opposite sides of the stereo mix, filling out the sound. However, if the parts aren't very precisely played it can just sound messy.

An alternative approach is that if guitar one is strumming, guitar two can do something different. Adding an arpeggio, as in this example, can sound more interesting than two guitars strumming along together.

PRO TIP

Playing an open string alongside the same note fretted gives you instant jangle. It will be easier to let that open string ring on if your fret-hand fingers are on their tips.

We are going to stay with arpeggios for while, and introduce the idea of a pedal note. A pedal is a musical term for a note that is held still while chords change. It can be a high note, a low note, or somewhere in between. In Exercise 63 the open E string is working as a pedal note from bar nine onwards. In Exercise 64, we have an E pedal all the way through, which is joined at bar nine by an open B pedal too. (Yes, you can have two at once.) We could call this repeated pattern a riff, though in more formal music circles it may be known as an 'ostinato.' For added jangle, the open E is doubled by the E at the fifth fret on the B string. Listen to the CD track – a pedal note creates tension as if the chords are anchored but trying to get away. The rhythm part in this track comes from Exercise 58, and the CD track has just rhythm and lead guitars. With a bassline in the rhythm part and arpeggios in the lead part you have a very filled-out sound – try getting it together with another guitar player. Swap parts when you repeat.

■ THEORY

The 'pedal' term originated in organ music, where you have bass pedals which are played with the feet. As we have seen, nowadays the pedal note does not have to be in the bass.

EXERCISE 64, CD TRACK 50 / 'Big Chords Two' (lead part)

(Chords from rhythm part)

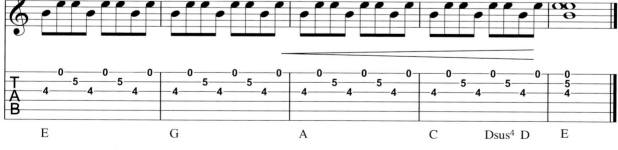

Exercise 65 uses a clean rich tone and arpeggios on open string chords in the style of REM guitarist Peter Buck. Some of the open string chord shapes are modified slightly as above; we don't need the whole chord, so unnecessary notes are left out. These shapes are worth practicing even if they are unfamiliar at first: economy of movement – not doing things you don't need to – is an important principle of advanced guitar playing.

Open-string chords for Exercise 65

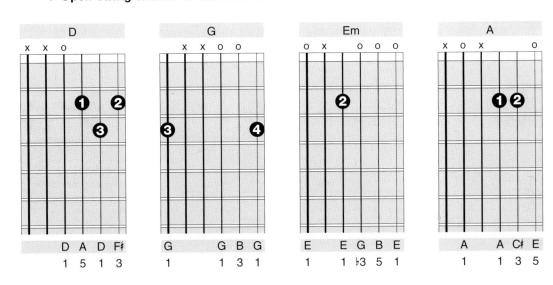

You may have noticed that this example is not in the usual 4/4, the four beat rhythm that pervades almost all rock music. Here we're in 6/8 time, which involves counting six eighth-note beats in each bar, but with accents on beats one and four – like this:

<u>1</u>   **2**   **3**   **<u>4</u>**   **5**   **6**

Try tapping in time with your foot while counting the beats and then add a handclap on one and four to get the feel of this example. Then make up your own arpeggios using other chord shapes you know. You could also try adding the occasional connecting bassline like the ones you see here.

PRO TIP
Remember to let the notes ring on, and try using either alternate picking or sweep picking. We've already looked at alternate picking, but sweep picking is where you use consecutive downstrokes when your hand is moving in a downwards direction, and consecutive upstrokes when your hand is moving in an upwards direction. I use a mixture of both alternate and sweep picking on this tune; see which works for you.

EXERCISE 65, **CD TRACK 51** / 'Buck The Trend'

the electric guitar handbook

Staying with the indie style, let's try mixing up flowing melody notes with strummed chords. The chord shapes will all be familiar, but you might notice that the G chord omits the A-string, using the same shape as used in Exercise 64 above. When strumming this G shape, the A-string is damped with the underside of the finger that's holding down the third fret on the E-string. It's probably best to alternate-pick the single notes, keeping to the principle of downstrokes on the downbeats and upstrokes on the upbeats; the opening bars are given for you.

Exercise 66 includes some of the ideas we looked at in the previous section, such as moving the strumming around so that you are not always playing the whole chord. Also notice that the chord changes don't always happen on the first beat of the bar. At the end of bar two, the G chord arrives on the very last eighth-note and is tied to the first beat of the next bar; musicians often describe this type of syncopation, where a chord arrives early, as a 'push.'

PRO TIP
Do you know any songs that you currently strum but could instead play using arpeggios? Start with the root note of the chord and then add as many of the higher notes as you need to fill the bar. Create a repeatable pattern, and try it with the pick or fingerstyle.

EXERCISE 66, CD TRACK 52 / 'Faithless'

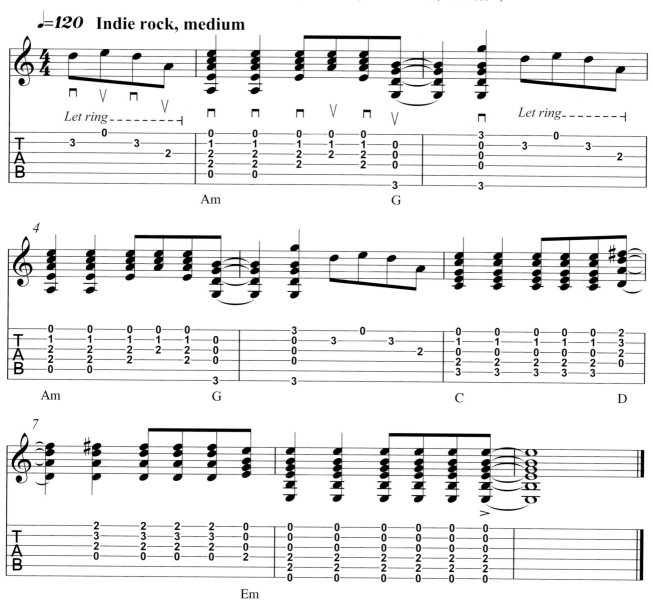

the electric guitar handbook

CHORDS AND ARPEGGIOS

EXERCISE 67, CD TRACK 53 / 'Stay The Same'

In Exercise 66 you may have noticed that the same four-note pattern kept coming back to start each phrase. Exercise 67, 'Stay The Same,' uses a similar approach to create a flowing arpeggio-based melodic line. The opening notes can be viewed as an arpeggio of a type of chord that's very useful in this jangly kind of rock music: a 'sus2' chord. We've already seen sus4 chords, and discussed the principles of building sus2 and sus4 chords in Exercise 55.

The first bar contains a pull-off from the second fret to the open E string; bar two has a slide from the second fret to the fourth fret on the G string. The first note of this slide is written in smaller size as it is a 'grace note' – a note which has no time of its own, but is very quickly followed by the main note (in this case, the fourth fret B).

An interesting feature of this piece is the way that the melody stays the same, while the chords change underneath. Some of the notes of this melody are chord-notes; for example, D, F-sharp, and A are in the chord of D major; but the melody notes E and B are the ninth and sixth and are outside the D major chord, but are interesting notes to add to it. When the chord changes to B minor the B now belongs to the chord, and the 'outside' notes are now E and A, which are the fourth and seventh. This means that although the melody is repeated several times its musical effect changes with each new chord.

PRO TIP

Using open strings whenever possible and letting notes ring on are important parts of this jangly arpeggio style.

CHORDS AND ARPEGGIOS

EXERCISE 68, **CD TRACK 54** / Rock arpeggios

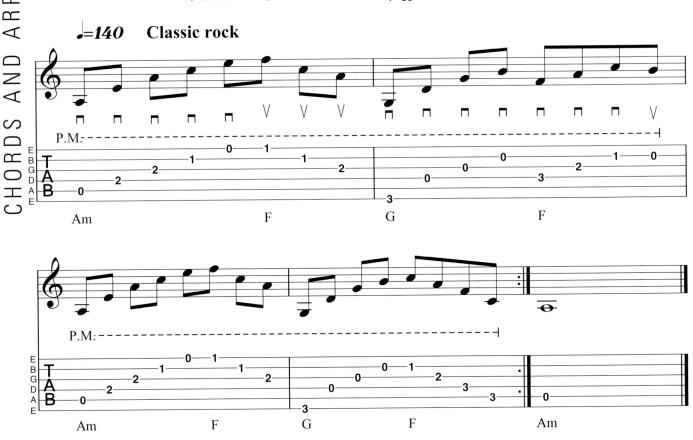

PRO TIP

Have you tried writing your own songs? Choose a few of the chords you know and see if they work well together. Try strums, arpeggios, riffs, and connecting notes to flesh out your guitar part in the ways that we've looked at. Write down or record any chord sequences that you make up that might be usable in a song.

Arpeggios are not only useful in jangly indie styles. With a touch of distortion and some palm muting they can be used very effectively in a rock context. Exercise 68 is based on three chords: A minor, G, and F (opposite). We have seen the A minor and G chords before, but the F major chord introduces a new technique; stopping two strings with one finger. In this case the first finger stops both the E and B strings at the first fret with what is known as a barre. (Nowadays this is often spelt 'bar' and usually rhymes with 'car'). When the barre is used to stop just a few strings it is often called a half-barre. A full barre is where the first finger stops all six strings.

This track is fairly fast and the palm muting adds to the level of difficulty, but it's really just a matter of getting your picking hand in the right place to mute the strings all the way across. Try using the pick directions that are given in the first two bars; they are based on the sweep picking principle of continuous downstrokes or upstrokes as appropriate. My personal preference for tracks like this is alternate picking. Try both and see which suits you best.

Bass riffs and connecting notes work just as well with arpeggios as with strummed chords. In Exercise 69 the music of Exercise 68 is re-used but with connecting riffs

the electric guitar handbook

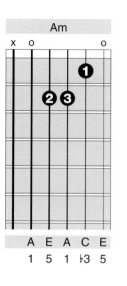
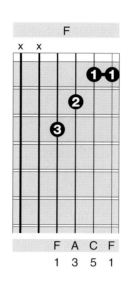
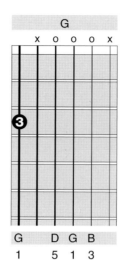

PRO TIP

When it comes to fingering, remember that although we are playing one note at a time the piece is based on chords. You should use sensible fingerings as if you were playing chord shapes, which should keep things tidy for the fret hand.

added in bars two and four. You have to briefly lift the palm mute for the riffs, and watch out for the hammer-on from open string to third fret in bar four. There is also a swirling phaser effect, which is combined with a rhythmic delay that pulses in time with the music. Experiment with these effects if you have them available.

EXERCISE 69, **CD TRACK 55** / Rock arpeggios two

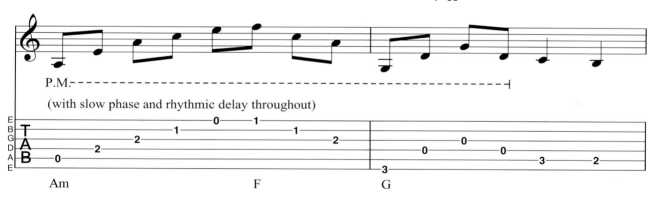

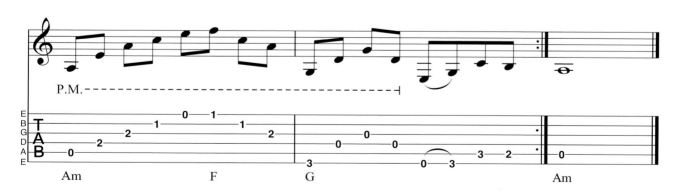

the electric guitar handbook

CHORD-BUILDING THREE

We have looked at building chords using roots, thirds, fifths and sevenths in Chord-Building One on page 102 and Chord-Building Two on page 116. We have also looked at keys and key signatures in Part One on page 70. Chords and keys are very closely related, and each major scale creates a unique sequence of chords. Let's start with a C major scale, and let each note of the scale be the root note of a chord. Then add the third and fifth above each root to create a series of triads.

We now have a sequence of seven chords all made from notes in the C major scale. Exercise 70 shows two possible fingerings for this sequence of chords; one that uses open strings whenever possible, and one that works its way up the neck keeping to the same three strings. Normally, we number these chords using Roman numerals: chords one, four, and five are major chords and are capitalised. Chords two, three, and six are minor and are lower case. Chord seven is diminished and is usually lower case.

Since every major scale has the same structure of tones and semitones, this

EXERCISE 70 / C major in triads

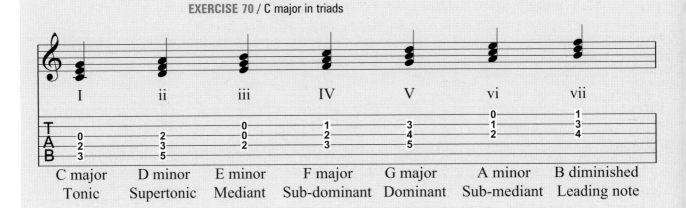

I	ii	iii	IV	V	vi	vii
C major	D minor	E minor	F major	G major	A minor	B diminished
Tonic	Supertonic	Mediant	Sub-dominant	Dominant	Sub-mediant	Leading note

pattern of major, minor, and diminished chords is the same for every major key. If we take G major, for example, we would say the chords in G major are:

G, A minor, B minor, C, D, E minor, and F-sharp diminished.

If you know what notes are in the major keys (see Part One page 72) you should be able to work out what chords are in every key.

In addition to a number, each step of the scale also has a name, as shown above. So we would say the dominant chord in C major is G major, or the sub-dominant chord in C major is F major. You will sometimes hear musicians using these technical terms when describing chord sequences. We might say, for example, that a piece of music 'starts on chord one and then goes to chord five.' We could also say it 'starts on the tonic and then goes to the dominant.' While these terms are not necessarily commonplace in the world of rock music, some familiarity with them could make the difference between looking clued-up and looking ill-informed.

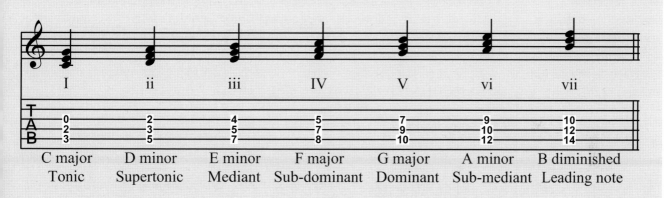

In Section Two of Part Two we have studied arpeggios big and small, introduced pedal notes and slides, and looked at ways of turning chord sequences into fully fleshed-out, interesting guitar parts. In the next section we will look at what we can do to make the chords themselves sound more interesting, using added notes and extensions.

EXTENDING CHORDS

extending chords

In this section we will look at added-note and extended chords; chords of this type are extremely common in modern rock music.

Let's start by learning the shapes below and playing the rhythm part that accompanies the lead guitar we first heard in Exercise 67 (CD track 53).

The B minor chord is our first proper bar chord, requiring the first finger of the fret hand to be laid straight across the second fret, stopping both the fifth string and the first string. Use the tip of the finger to mute the low E string. Asus4 should need no explanation as we have seen suspended fourth chords before. (The open first string can be sounded in Asus4 and A major, but in this piece I chose to mute it to give the melody more space above the rhythm part.) D/C is 'D with C bass.' This type of chord is usually known as a 'slash' chord, and is used when we wish to specify a bass note other than the root for a chord.

Chord grids are given on the score, and the strumming is a very straightforward repeated pattern that we have come across before.

PRO TIP

Compare the B minor shape to your open A minor shape. Can you see the connection between them? The B minor is the A minor shape played two frets higher up the guitar using the barre where before we had open strings.

Chords for Exercise 71

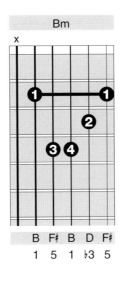

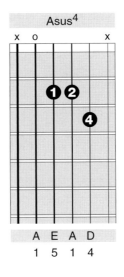

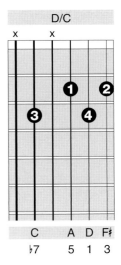

EXERCISE 71, CD TRACK 53 / 'Stay The Same' (rhythm part)

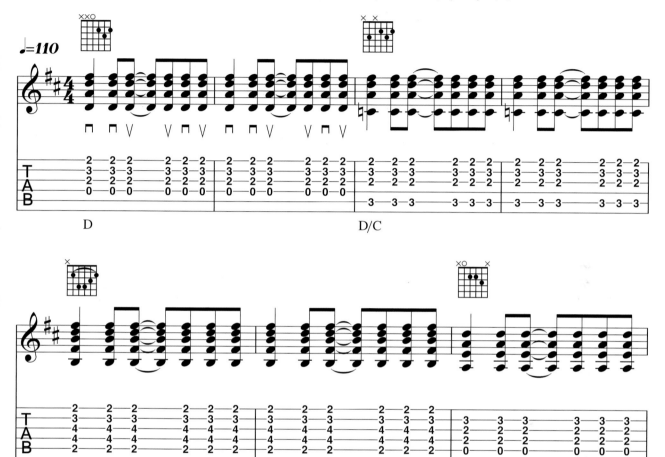

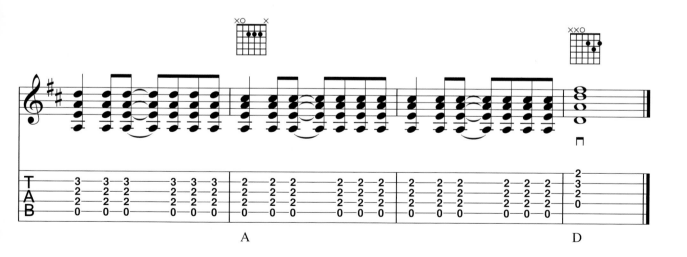

Chords for Exercise 72

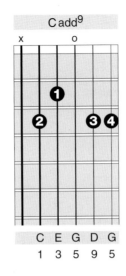

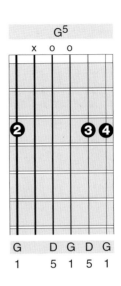

PRO TIP

Notice that in bars three, four, seven, eight and many others we have chords that are 'pushed' or syncopated as we have discussed in earlier exercises.

In Exercise 72, 'Fives And Nines,' we have modified the C and G open-string chords that we learned in Section One. The C chord has an added D on the B-string and G on the top E-string. The added D is the ninth letter name up from C and gives the chord its name, Cadd9. (The G is a fifth and belongs in the chord already).

The G chord has been changed by leaving notes out. The B on the A string is now muted, and the B open string has a D at the third fret. This leaves us with nothing but Gs and Ds, or roots and fifths, so the chord is called G5. This chord has a distinctive 'jangly but empty' quality that suits many kinds of rock music. When we add Dsus4 to the sequence we find we have three chords that share the same two top notes – interesting!

The piece begins with held chords and fairly spacious strumming, before moving into a busier, accented strum at bar nine. The dot above the first chord in bars nine and ten is a 'staccato' sign; if you listen to the CD track you will hear that that chord is cut short as well as accented. Bars nine to 12 are repeated and at bar 13 we settle on a D major chord for the last four bars, which we call a 'coda' – which literally means a 'tail' – or an ending section. We will learn a lead part to this track in Part Three.

This track was inspired by the rhythm tracks to songs by bands like AC/DC and Guns N' Roses.

EXTENDING CHORDS

EXERCISE 72, **CD TRACK 56** / 'Fives And Nines' (rhythm part)

the electric guitar handbook

EXTENDING CHORDS

MORE EXTENDED CHORDS

All these shapes are modified versions of the open-string chords that we learned back at the beginning of Section One. The easiest way to memorize them is to compare them to the chords you already know and get used to the added notes and the extended shapes. In fact, these are just some of the possibilities, and you may be able to experiment with other open-string chords and come up with interesting and original sounds of your own.

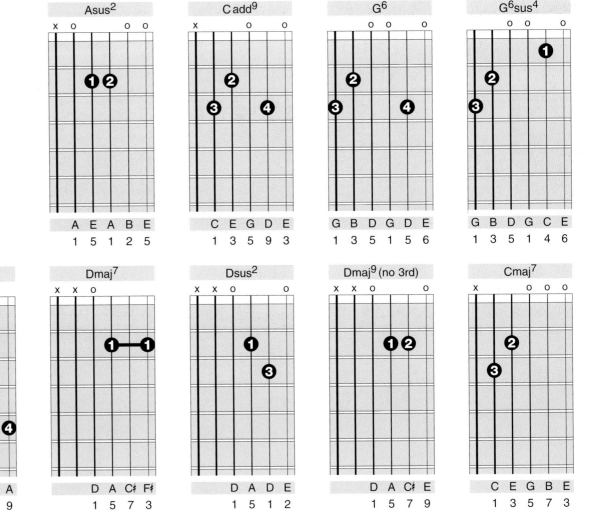

Asus^2

A E A B E
1 5 1 2 5

Cadd^9

C E G D E
1 3 5 9 3

G^6

G B D G D E
1 3 5 1 5 6

G^{6}sus^4

G B D G C E
1 3 5 1 4 6

Gadd^9

G D G B A
1 5 1 3 9

Dmaj^7

D A C♯ F♯
1 5 7 3

Dsus^2

D A D E
1 5 1 2

Dmaj^9 (no 3rd)

D A C♯ E
1 5 7 9

Cmaj^7

C E G B E
1 3 5 7 3

■ THEORY

As you add notes to chords it can be tricky to come up with accurate names for your new shape. The best thing is to keep a pencil and paper handy and get used to drawing quick chord diagrams. Then think of a name that means something to you like 'D with added G.' It is more important that the name means something to you than that it is technically accurate. You will find the chords I've shown here in various songs and chord books, and sometimes they'll have different names – which goes to show that guitar players often disagree about the 'correct' names for some complex chords. So don't get hung up on names at this stage. Just enjoy these chiming, resonant sounds and see if you can come up with some chord sequences of your own that use them.

Exercise 73 uses extended chords to create melodies in strummed chords. There are three separate examples using the shapes above; each one is played twice. You will probably have no problem working out the strumming, but will need to be accurate

EXERCISE 73, **CD TRACK 57** / Extended chord shapes

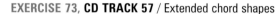

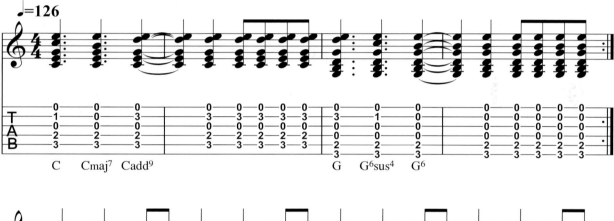

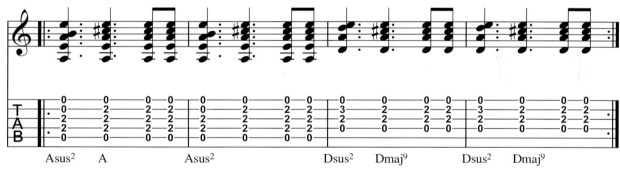

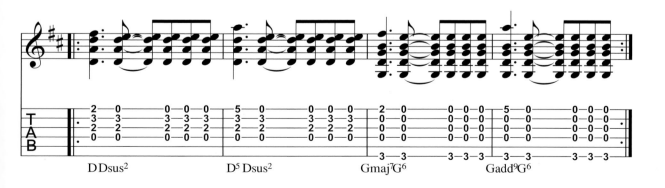

the electric guitar handbook

with your fret-hand fingers to allow fretted notes and open string notes to sound together. Listen carefully to your chords to make sure all the notes are sounding.

If you've heard bands like R.E.M., Coldplay, Radiohead, The Smiths, and so on you'll have heard this type of playing. Back in the 1960s, The Who's Pete Townshend also played rhythm parts that made use of extended chord shapes. These types of jangly guitar chord have become key ingredients in the sounds of indie bands today.

It's time to go deeper into the wonderful world of bar chords. For reference purposes we have the B minor shape again, and are also introducing an A major chord at the fifth fret and a G major chord at the third fret. One of the exciting things about bar chords is that they are movable; you might notice that the A major and G major shapes

Open-string and added-note chords for Exercise 74

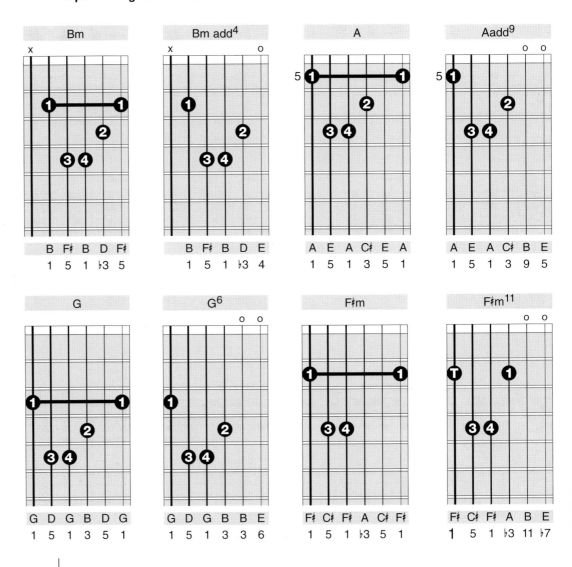

the electric guitar handbook

are the same but played at different frets. You could play this shape at any fret and name the chord from the note you were holding down on the sixth string. The second fret F-sharp minor chord is also movable, and would also take its name from whichever note was held down on the sixth string. The B minor shape is movable, and this time the root (or name-note) is on the fifth string.

Alongside these bar chords we have some added-note chords that can be played by releasing the barre and adding the top E, or E and B, open strings. Isn't it great that sometimes you can find great new sounds by using fewer, rather than more fingers? Start by strumming these shapes in turn and listen closely to make sure all the notes are ringing clearly. Experiment with these shapes together with those in previous examples, and see what you come up with. Try one chord per bar at first, but don't be afraid of changing chord more often if it sounds good to you. Note that the last chord shown, F#m11, uses your thumb over the neck on the sixth string. If you can't get your thumb over just leave that bass note out; either damp the string with your thumb or be careful not to strum it.

Exercise 74 (next page) uses all eight of the above chord diagrams to create a piece in the style of Coldplay. It begins with held bar chords; a chance to practice moving those tricky shapes around. Then we move into a chugging downstroke rhythm with accents on beats two, three, and four – watch out for the repeat signs. At bar 13, there is a rise in dynamic level (ie, it gets louder), and we begin using the added note chords as seen above; again, this section is repeated before we wind things down with more held chords, this time of the added-note variety. If you look at the notation stave from bar 13 onwards you'll see that when notes are stacked close together in chords, one note sometimes has to be offset slightly – you still play all these notes at once.

DYNAMICS

Abrupt changes in the dynamic level of music are written in italic script using the letters *p* and *f*, which stand for piano and forte – literally soft and hard. In between the extremes of quiet and loud we have *mezzo piano* (*mp*) and *mezzo forte* (*mf*).

There are eight of these signs in common use; here they are in order, going from extremely quiet to extremely loud:

ppp   pp   p   mp   mf   f   ff   fff

In bar eight we have the sign *p*, as the chord in that bar is played more softly than the others. Bar nine sees a return to *mf*, before a boost in the level at bar 13 with *f*. In bar 17 we return to *mf*, with the final two chords in bars 21 and 22 played *p*. Dynamic signs like these are not particularly common in rock music but you should know what they mean in case you ever come across them.

---

the electric guitar handbook

EXTENDING CHORDS

EXERCISE 74, **CD TRACK 58** / Bar chords and added notes

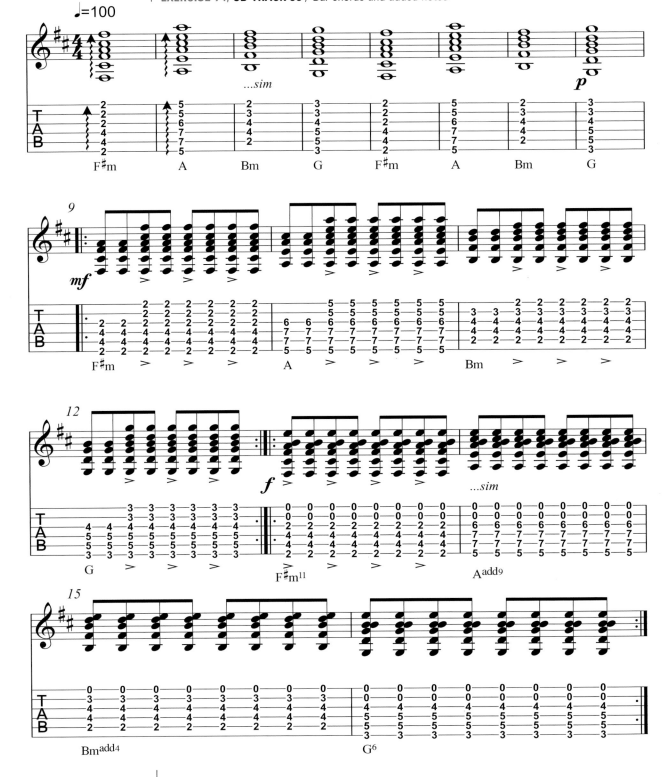

EXERCISE 74 *continued*

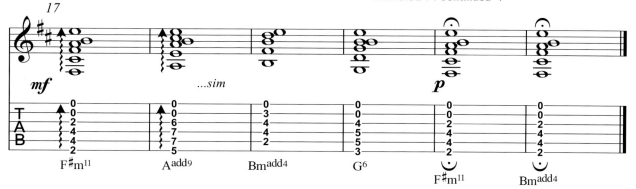

F#m11   Aadd9   Bmadd4   G6   F#m11   Bmadd4

■ THEORY

There is one other new sign in this music. This is known as a 'pause' or, to use its technical name, a 'fermata.' It can be seen above the chords in bars 21 and 22, and it means that you should break with the regular pulse and play these chords freely as appropriate.

Before we move on to more movable chords and exploring the neck a little, here are a few more extended chords that every guitar player should know. A major seventh chord is made up of a major triad with an added major seventh. A minor seventh chord is made up of a minor triad with an added minor seventh. Look closely at these chord diagrams, so that you understand which note is the root, the third, the fifth, or the seventh for each shape. Practice each chord in turn, and compare it with the plain major or minor chord on which it is based.

Major seventh chords

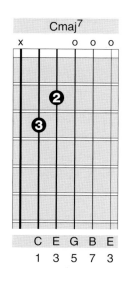

Cmaj7

C E G B E
1 3 5 7 3

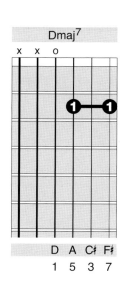

Dmaj7

D A C# F#
1 5 3 7

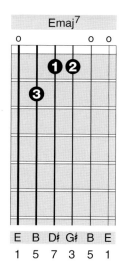

Emaj7

E B D# G# B E
1 5 7 3 5 1

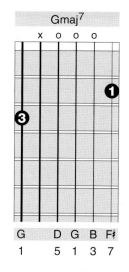

Gmaj7

G   D G B F#
1   5 1 3 7

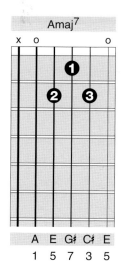

Amaj7

A E G# C# E
1 5 7 3 5

EXTENDING CHORDS

Minor seventh chords

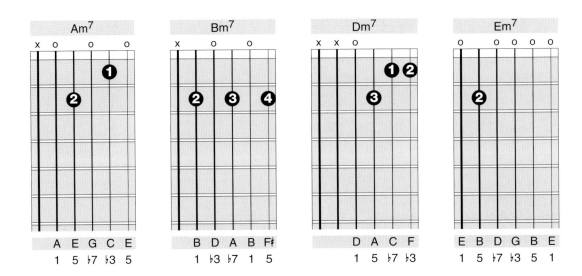

Major seventh chords have a soft and dreamy quality; minor sevenths have a jazzy flavour not found in the plain minor chord. Exercise 75 consists of some chord sequences that use these chords and others that we already know. Play them in any rhythm you like; the idea is just to get you started using these shapes. Then experiment and see if you can make up some of your own chord sequences using these shapes. Aim for four-bar or eight-bar structures and see if you can fit them together in arrangements using one sequence as a verse and another sequence as a chorus. Mix in plain majors and minors, some extended chords and seventh chords too, if you like their sound, and you'll soon be songwriting.

In Section Three we have expanded our knowledge of chord construction and learned many new chords, using sevenths, added ninths, sixths and so on. We have also learned about slash chords and sus chords and looked at ways of using these new shapes to add interest to chord sequences. In the next section we go further into movable chords and begin to explore the dusty end of the guitar neck.

the electric guitar handbook

Strum ad lib

EXERCISE 75 / Major and minor seventh chords

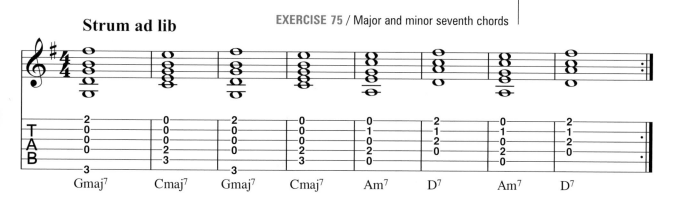

Gmaj⁷ Cmaj⁷ Gmaj⁷ Cmaj⁷ Am⁷ D⁷ Am⁷ D⁷

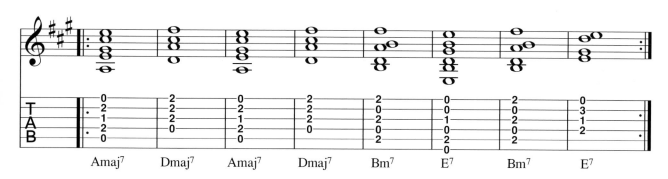

Amaj⁷ Dmaj⁷ Amaj⁷ Dmaj⁷ Bm⁷ E⁷ Bm⁷ E⁷

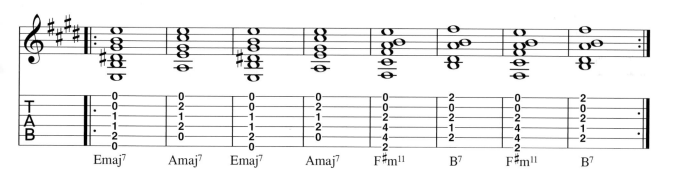

Emaj⁷ Amaj⁷ Emaj⁷ Amaj⁷ F♯m¹¹ B⁷ F♯m¹¹ B⁷

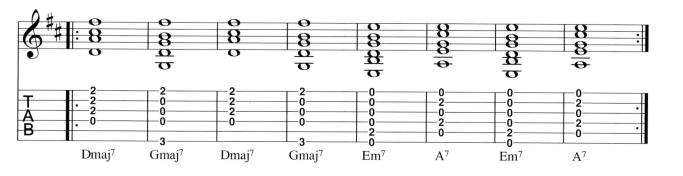

Dmaj⁷ Gmaj⁷ Dmaj⁷ Gmaj⁷ Em⁷ A⁷ Em⁷ A⁷

the electric guitar handbook

movable chords

In Section Four we will be looking at triads and diads that can be moved around and played anywhere on the neck. To begin with, we need to return to the subject of building chords and learn about inversions.

■ THEORY

When using Roman numerals to describe chords in a key we add the letter 'a' for a root position chord (eg, IVa), 'b' for a first inversion (eg, IVb) and 'c' for a second inversion (eg, IVc). These symbols are used mainly when performing harmonic analysis of a piece of music and as a result are not common in rock music; at least you'll know what they are if you ever come across them.

CHORD-BUILDING FOUR

The strongest sounding bass note for a chord is the root. Put quite simply, chords 'sound best' with the root note in the bass. However, we have already seen that you can add a bass note to a chord in the form of slash chords. It is also possible to have chords 'the wrong way up,' with the third or the fifth in the bass. A chord with the third in the bass is known as a first inversion; a chord with the fifth in the bass is known as a second inversion.

Root position

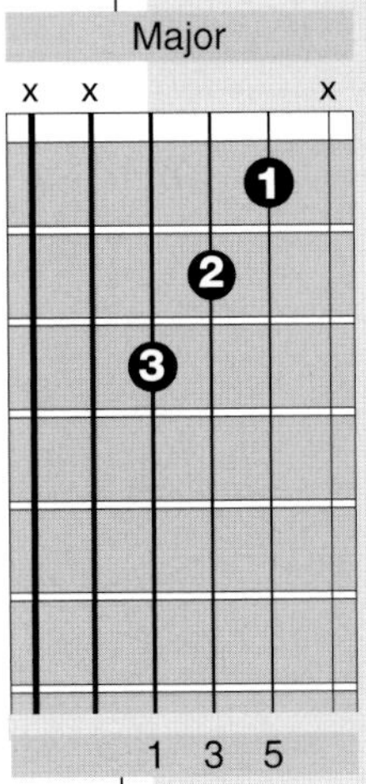

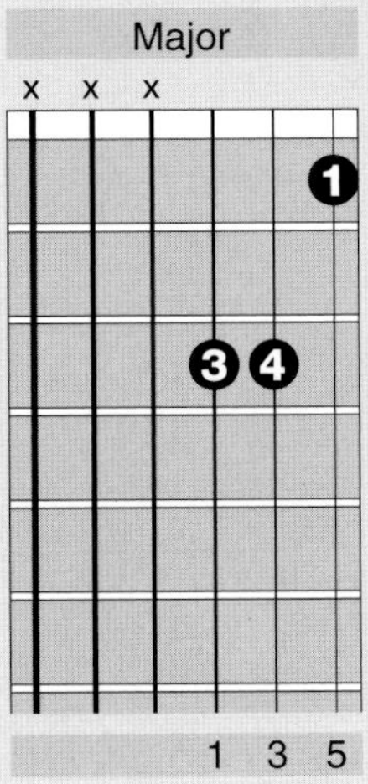

First inversion

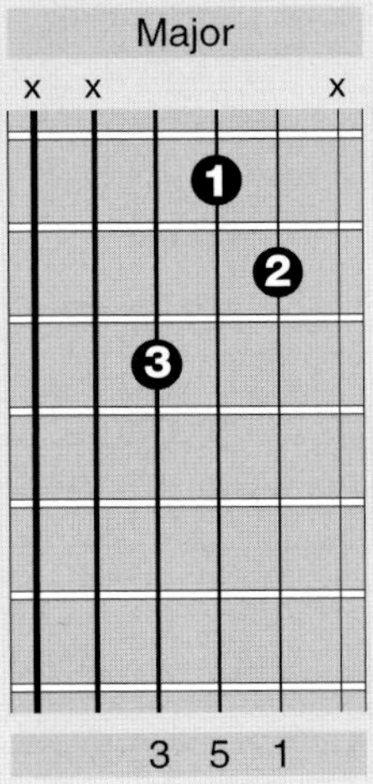

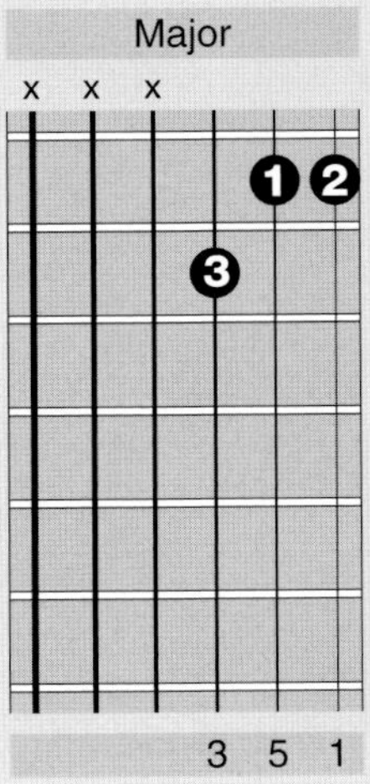

| Major | Major | Major | Major |
| 1 3 5 | 1 3 5 | 3 5 1 | 3 5 1 |

Exercise 76, 'Positive Pedal,' uses the triad shapes we've been looking at to play a rock-style rhythm part over a bass-guitar pedal note. The E pedal note occurs in most of the triads, which helps this style of playing to work, though it is possible for the bass note not to be in any of the chords. The name of each triad is given underneath each chord shape. Can you work out which of the three notes is the root, and which inversion we are using? Use the note map at the back of the book to help you figure out the note names high up on the neck. Work on the changes one at a time if you find them tricky, and remember to keep your fingers close to the strings.

You can find playing like this in many classic tracks. The guitar part to The Who's 'Can't Explain' is built on triads. The intro to the Rolling Stones' 'Brown Sugar' adds a pedal note, as does the intro to the chorus of Van Halen's 'Running with the Devil.'

PRO TIP

Exercice's 76 guitar part uses mostly downstrokes for added rhythmic drive. Mute the top E-string with the underside of your first finger so that it won't sound when you strum.

Here are six diagrams that show the chord shapes for root position, first inversion, and second inversion major triads on the D, G, and B strings, and also on the G, B, and E strings. All of these shapes are movable – they can be played at any fret. The best way to use them is to memorise both the shape and which note of the shape is the root. Remember that the chords take their name from the root note. For example, if you were to play the first shape with your third finger on the G that is on the D string at the fifth fret, you would be playing a G major triad in root position. This will probably be clearer after the following example.

Second inversion

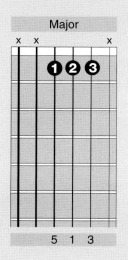

Major

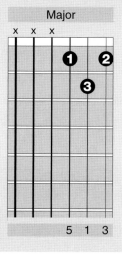

Major

MOVABLE CHORDS

EXERCISE 76, **CD TRACK 59** / 'Positive Pedal'

(E pedal throughout)

The rhythm part to 'Movable Metal,' which we first heard as Exercise 28, CD Track 20, uses a different kind of movable chord. The 5 chords we learned at the end of Part One all involved an open string, but the shape can be modified to create a diad that can be played at any fret. The piece starts on the open E5 chord, which should be familiar, and this is then followed by some straightforward 5 chord riffs using the moveable 5 chord shape. There is a 'stop' in the middle of the track which is very much part of the modern metal style. Count the four beats of the empty bar in your head and you should be able to come back in with the backing track if you're playing along. Use

the electric guitar handbook

EXERCISE 77, CD TRACK 20 / 'Movable Metal' (rhythm part)

the electric guitar handbook

Movable 5 chords

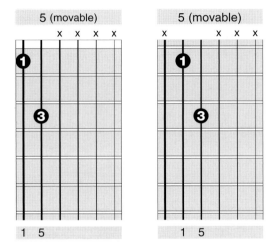

fingers one and three and keep your fret-hand fingers on the strings, sliding smoothly between the shapes. Eventually you'll be able to keep the fingers apart as you slide.

■ THEORY

These 5 chord shapes work with the root on the D or fourth string too.

Staying with movable 5 chords for a while, in Exercise 78 we are going to experiment with a slight retuning of the guitar. In drop D tuning you take your low E string down a whole tone to D. A quick way of doing this is to play a your E and D strings at the same time and then crank the E tuner down until the notes are an octave apart. You won't have to move it far. This tuning gives you D, A, and D as your lowest three strings

Three-note movable 5 chords

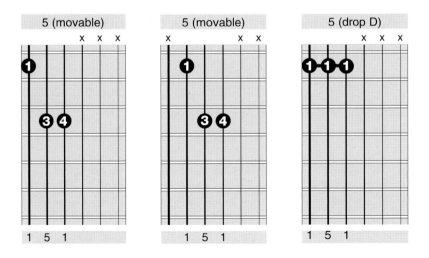

MOVABLE CHORDS

EXERCISE 78, **CD TRACK 60** / 'Drop D'

♩=92   **Metal - medium and heavy**

Drop D tuning

Repeat and fade.....

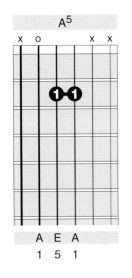

A⁵

AEA
1 5 1

– in other words, a D5 chord as a three note shape with the root doubled at the bottom and the top of the chord. You can play this 5 chord shape anywhere on the lower three strings using just one finger, and you won't need to look far to find tracks by metal or indie bands using this approach.

'Drop D' is inspired by the track 'Sad But True' from Metallica's *Black* album, and shows the fun you can have playing in drop D tuning and using this simple chord shape. Watch out for the sudden stops, staccatos, and the pull-offs in bars nine to 12. And don't forget to tune your E-string back up before you move on to the next exercise.

TUNING

Back in the 1960s, Jimi Hendrix often tuned his guitar one half-step down from regular EADGBE to E♭A♭D♭G♭B♭E♭, and many other guitarists (Eddie Van Halen, Stevie Ray Vaughan, etc) have followed his lead. It gives the guitar a looser feel and generally deepens the tone, although Jimi also found singing easier in the lower key. If you try this 'step down' tuning you could then do drop-D (or drop D-flat as it would be), which many metal bands use. Some bands take their tuning down a whole step, to DGCFAD, and then do drop-D, or drop-C as we could call it. Seven-string guitars, with a low B

EXERCISE 79, CD TRACK 61 / A5 plus riff

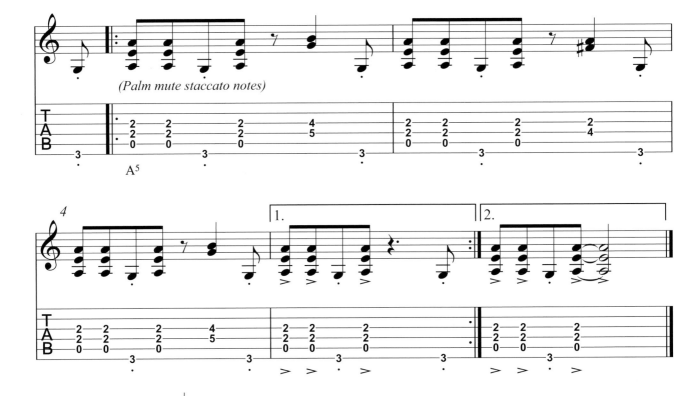

(Palm mute staccato notes)

A⁵

string added to the regular six, became popular in the 1990s, but most of what can be achieved with a seven-string can be done with a detuned six-string.

In standard tuning, the three-note A5 chord (left) can be played down the lower end of the guitar with just one finger, and in this rock-inspired example (Exercise 79) we are combining it with palm-muted bass notes and a two-note (diad) descending pattern. The diads are in fact the lower two notes of the triad shapes we looked at earlier. This example shows that 5 chords and triads can be mixed together to make a satisfying rhythm part.

PRO TIP

Be careful with the palm muting – aim just to mute the notes on the low E-string, not the A5 chord.

EXERCISE 80, **CD TRACK 62** / Grunge-style riffs

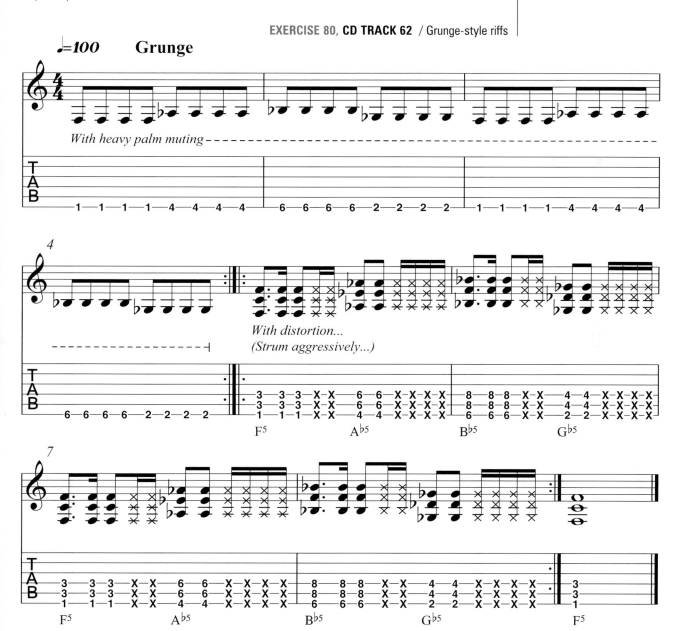

the electric guitar handbook

Three-note 5 chords

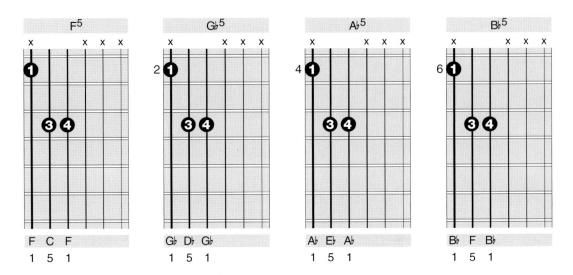

If you've been working on moving your 5 chords around, as in Exercises 77 and 78, you should also be able to cope with moving this three-note shape around. This piece is inspired by the track 'Smells Like Teen Spirit' by Nirvana. It begins with heavily muted bass notes, slid around the guitar. You could try a really basic approach and play this part with just your first finger – this is the quiet 'verse' section. Then release the palm mute and give it all you've got for the 5-chord 'chorus' section. If you find it hard to move this three-note shape around quickly, you could always begin by practicing it with the two-note 5 chord and then move on to the three-note version when you're ready. Release the fret-hand pressure to use fret-hand muting when you play the notes written as 'XXX.'

Back in Part One, Section Four, we learned to vamp on A, D, and E, alternating between A5 and A6, or D5 and D6, etc, using shapes with an open string as the root. We know that 5 chords can be movable, and with a movable 6th chord we will be able to play a 12-bar blues vamp in any key. There is a stretch involved in reaching from the fifth to the ninth fret for the A6 and D6 chords, but if you open your hand and relax

PRO TIP

When moving chords like this around it is better to look at where your hand is going than where your hand is at the moment. If you look ahead and focus on the target fret you will find it easier to move your hand accurately to the next position.

A5/A6 vamp

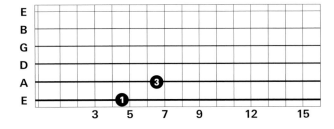
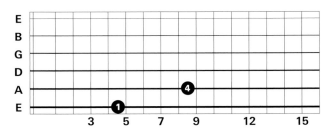

MOVABLE CHORDS

EXERCISE 81, CD TRACK 63 / 'Steady As A Rock' vamp

MOVABLE CHORDS

D5/D6 vamp

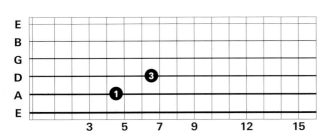

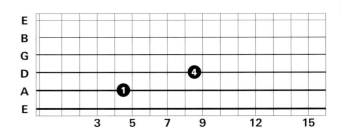

rather than use force you should get the hang of it before too long. In this example the E5/E6 chords are played using the open E root. If you moved the D shapes up two frets you could play E5/E6 at the seventh fret instead.

The rhythm guitar part is panned slightly to the right of centre – you should be able to hear it if you listen closely. We'll study the lead guitar part in Part Three, Section Two.

PRO TIP
Blues and related styles mainly use chords I, IV, and V, which in this key (A major) are A, D, and E. Can you work out what I, IV and V would be in the other common keys, such as C, D, E, F, G and B-flat? Play the blues in all these keys if you can.

In this section we have looked at triads and their inversions and at moving these shapes around the guitar. We have also introduced movable 5 chords and the idea of playing a blues vamp in any key. Part Two as a whole is a thorough and detailed introduction to playing chords on the guitar. If you found some of the exercises difficult, you should keep returning to them, practicing slowly and carefully and with patience. If you've come this far, you should be proud of your progress and looking forward to Part Three, where we return to lead guitar.

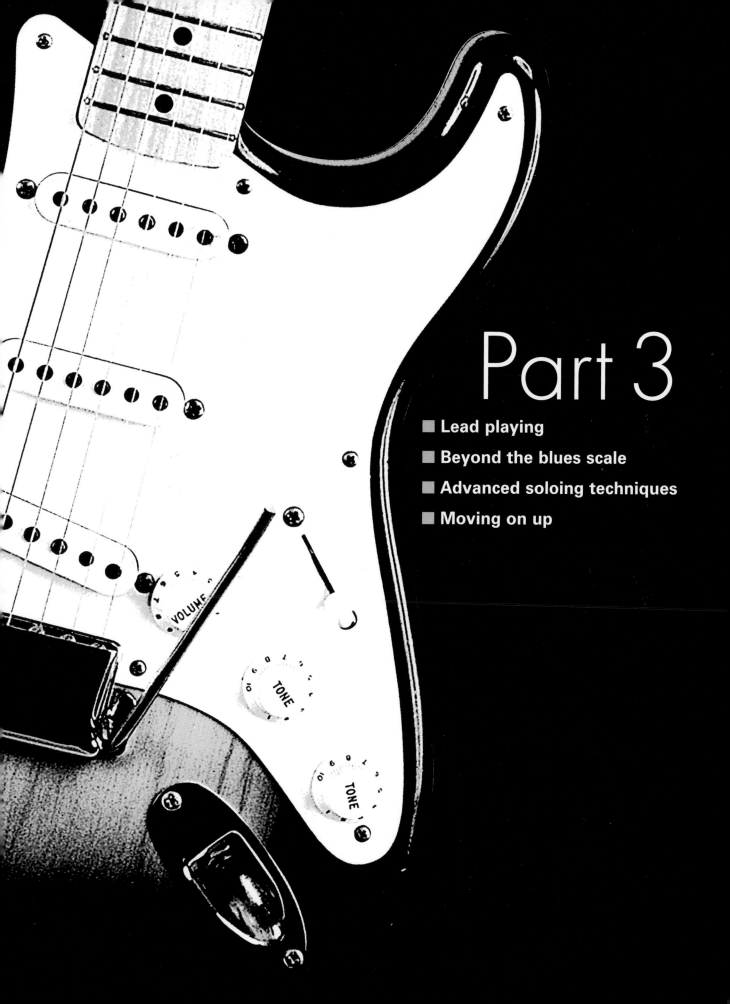

Part 3

- Lead playing
- Beyond the blues scale
- Advanced soloing techniques
- Moving on up

lead playing

In the early stages of Part Three we are going to concentrate on single-note lead guitar playing. Chords will never be far away, however, and we will learn the rhythm or chord parts to the examples whenever there is a second guitar part. We will then have two-guitar arrangements that you can work on with a partner if you wish.

Exercise 82, 'Chili California,' is a piece that has two very different sections. The first eight bars combine elements of chord and arpeggio playing with single-note playing. There is a sustained bass note at the start of each bar and a melody that combines chord-notes and passing-notes. This contrasts with bars eight to 16, which are a busy, lightweight strum. The music is based on A minor, F major, and G major, and these familiar shapes are given below, but you don't actually need them to play the first eight bars – the shapes are given so that you can compare them to the tab and see how the music is based on each chord. The second section uses the above chords but with the alteration of the F major chord to Fmaj7. You will need to hold the pick lightly and strum the strings evenly to get the right effect here.

This Red Hot Chili Peppers-style piece can be tricky to play, mainly because the first section is really two pieces of music at once, with melody and bass notes all played on one guitar. Be sure to let both parts ring on and let the melody notes overlap the bass notes. This was played with the pick throughout, but you could try fingerstyle at the beginning, with your thumb on the bass notes, and index and middle fingers on the melody.

Chords for 'Chili California'

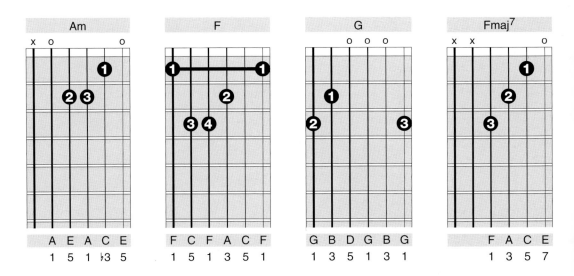

Am	F	G	Fmaj7
A E A C E	F C F A C F	G B D G B G	F A C E
1 5 1 ♭3 5	1 5 1 3 5 1	1 3 5 1 3 1	1 3 5 7

EXERCISE 82, **CD TRACK 64** / 'Chili California'

■ THEORY

If you take a close look at the notation stave in the first eight bars you will see music written in two parts for the first time in this book. The bass line is written 'tails down' and all the notes have their full value, adding up to a complete bar. Above them the melody part is written 'tails up' and again adds up to a complete bar. So we have two complete 'parts' at once.

PRO TIP

Compare the riff in each bar to the chord shapes above and work out which notes are in the chord and which are passing notes. Try making up your own riffs in this style using this as a starting point.

As the strumming gets going in bar nine, the lead guitar part joins in with a simple melody played in the fifth position, with finger one at the fifth fret and the fingers spanning frets five to eight. See opposite top for the notes in the fifth position. The piece begins with eight bars of silence while the rhythm guitar plays the introduction; it's a good idea to practice counting your way through these empty bars as you never know when you might need this skill. The notes come from the A minor pentatonic

EXERCISE 83, CD TRACK 64 / 'Chili California' lead part

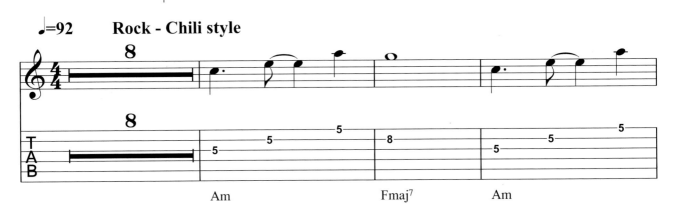

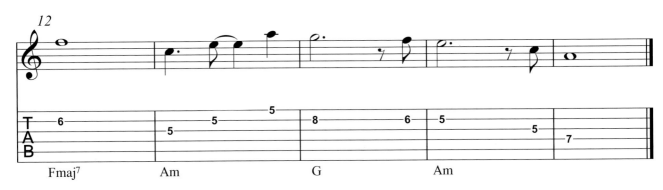

Notes in fifth position

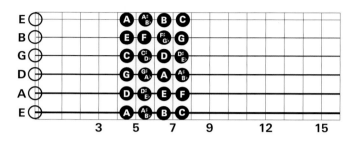

scale, (see the next exercise) with the addition of the occasional F on the sixth fret of the B-string. The first bar should be played entirely with finger one, beginning with it on its tip on the G-string, and then lying it down as you play the B-string and the E-string. Use all four fret-hand fingers to play this piece, using one finger per fret.

Back in part one we learned the blues scale in E, starting on the open low E string. If we re-finger the blues scale, avoiding open strings, we have a movable shape that we can play at any fret and in any key. The scale is illustrated here starting on A at the fifth fret, in both notation/tab (over the page) and graphic form. The minor pentatonic is also illustrated graphically, showing that it only differs from the blues scale by omitting the flattened fifth.

This movable blues scale is probably the most useful scale shape you will ever learn. There are hundreds of guitar solos and riffs that are based entirely upon this scale, and there are thousands of solos that begin on this shape or refer to it at some point. Play the scale keeping to the 'one finger per fret' rule, and use alternate picking; down, up, down, up. You will find that it is tempting to use an extra downstroke as you change strings when you are going up, and to use an extra upstroke as you change strings when you are coming back down. The scale will sound smoother and you will be able to play it faster if you use alternate picking.

Blues scale and minor pentatonic scale

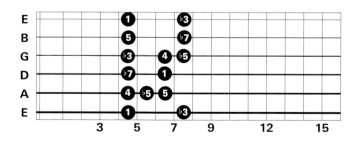
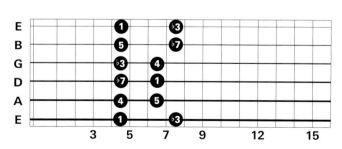

EXERCISE 84, CD TRACK 65 / Two-octave blues scale in A

Exercise 85 uses the blues scale to create riffs which are then played in the style of an improvised solo over three choruses of 12-bar blues in A.

Chorus one: notice that the first short phrase is repeated, and is then played again in bars seven and eight, where it acts as an 'answer' to the 'question' in bars five and six. It returns again in bars in 11 and 12, where it is an answer to the question in bars nine and ten. 'Question and answer' phrasing is an important ingredient in building solos and melodies, and not just in the blues.

Chorus two: chorus two introduces a new riff which is used in the same way. Notice that there is plenty of space in these solos; there's no need to play all the time or try to fill up every bar. Try making up your own solo, and remember to practice phrasing, letting your solo evolve from a few simple riffs. In bars 17 and 18 the riff

the electric guitar handbook

EXERCISE 85, CD TRACK 66 / Blues riffs

continued over page

the electric guitar handbook

LEAD PLAYING

EXERCISE 85 *continued*

EXERCISE 85 continued

from bars five and six in chorus one is repeated. It's good to re-use material from earlier in a solo.

Chorus three: once again a new riff is established in bars 25 to 28, and then used question-and-answer style in the remaining bars. On the CD, the lead guitar is panned hard left, so that it can be isolated or cut out altogether if you want to practice your own ideas over the blues sequence. Try recording yourself playing the rhythm track from Exercise 81 and then practice soloing over the backing track you've made. To make these solos easier to play there are no slides, slurs, or bends included; none of the stuff that makes the guitar wail and sing! That's coming up later in this section.

In Exercise 84 we learned the movable blues scale in the key of A. We call it movable because it can be played at any fret, and to prepare for the next example (Exercise 87) we are going to play the blues scale starting at the third fret in the key of G. Just in case you're confused by this, the scale is written out here for you in the new key. You should be able to figure this out for yourself now, so this example is not on the CD.

EXERCISE 86 / Blues scale in G

the electric guitar handbook

LEAD PLAYING

EXERCISE 87, CD TRACK 67 / 'Funky Junction'

♩=80   **Funky 16s**

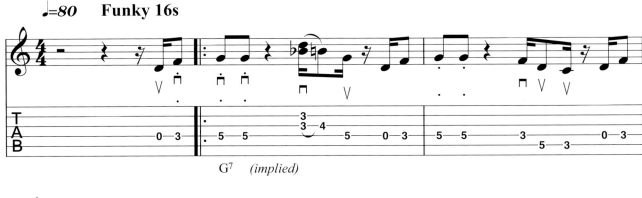

G⁷   *(implied)*

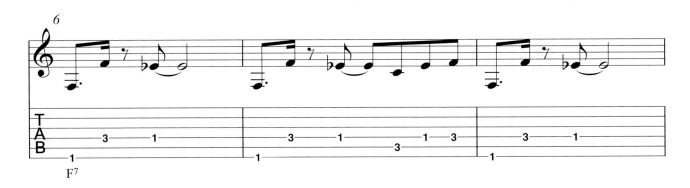

F⁷

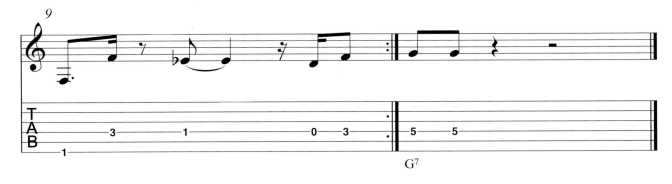

G⁷

the electric guitar handbook

Exercise 87, 'Funky Junction,' is in fact based on two blues scales; G for the first four bars and F for the last four bars. When you have figured it out, check out these scales and see how they relate to the notes of the piece. Maybe you could work out a piece of your own using a similar approach.

The piece begins with a two-note lead-in that comes just before the first downbeat, and there is an underlying funky 16th-note rhythm. Watch out for the cool hammer-on lick in bars two and four, which involves stopping the G and B strings at the third fret with finger one and then hammering on at the fourth fret on the G string with finger two. If you have been following our ongoing study of chords and intervals you will know that this hammer-on takes you from B-flat, the minor third, to B-natural, the major third. This works well as it fits the underlying chord of G7.

The second guitar part in this example (Exercise 88) drives the rhythm along with some choppy chords. The G7 chord is played under the G blues scale riff, and the F7 chord is played under the F blues scale riff. Notice that the blues scale is essentially minor in character (it has a minor third) but that it is very often used to play over rhythm parts with a major character, made up of major chords that have a major third. This clash between the minor third of the scale and the major third of the chord is an essential part of the blues sound. The XXX notes are muted with the fret hand – release the pressure but don't take the fingers all the way off the strings. You might recognize the chord shape we're using; it is the C7 open string chord moved up the neck. This chord is moveable as long as you mute the top and bottom strings with the underside of finger one and the tip of finger three. It's a great chord shape that fits the hand nicely and makes a strong and compact sound.

PRO TIP
Recognizing a pattern in the music, for instance that it is based on the blues scale, can speed up the learning process.

F7 and G7 chords for Exercise 88

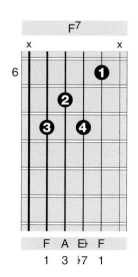
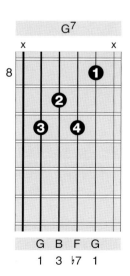

LEAD PLAYING

EXERCISE 88, CD TRACK 67 / 'Funky Junction' rhythm part

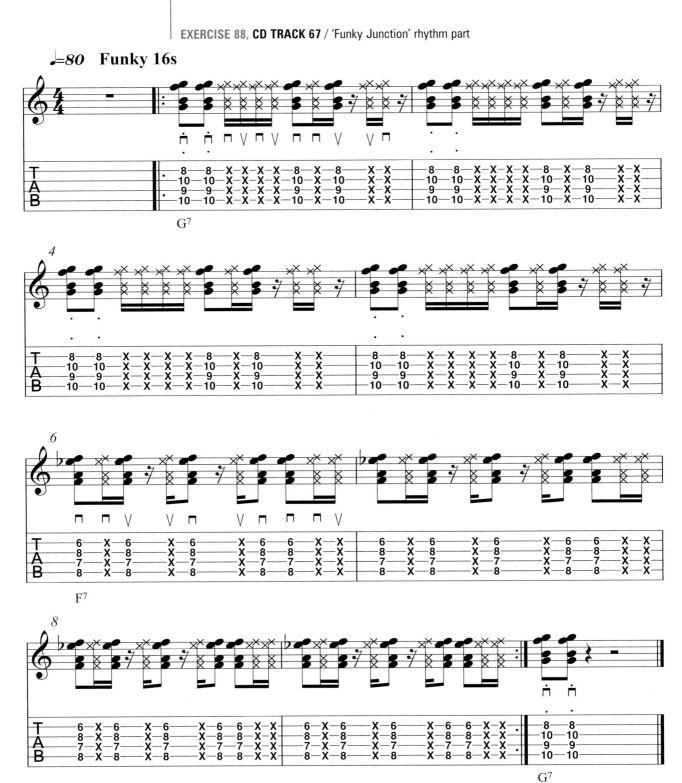

The piece is based around two rhythms – one for the G7 chord and one for the F7 chord. On the repeat the playing is a little looser so feel free to stretch out and improvise with the rhythm as your confidence grows.

■ THEORY

If you take a close look at the chord diagrams you will see that the fifth is omitted from these chords, as they have only root, third, seventh, and root again. It's okay to leave out the fifth in this shape as the main sound of the chord comes from the diminished fifth between the third and seventh.

We have already looked at techniques such as slides and slurs that can make the guitar expressive, so in Exercise 89 we are going to add the best one of all: the bend.

Take a look at Example 1. Place your third finger on the seventh fret of the G-string, play the note and then push the string in an upward direction (towards the D-string). You should hear it rise in pitch. It will be easier if you help finger three by placing your first and second fingers on the string and pushing with them as well. You are aiming to make the string rise two frets in pitch; the upward pointing arrow on the tab stave is the sign for a bend, and the word 'full' means a whole step (two half-steps/semitones) rise in pitch. On the notation stave a bend is notated as an angled line between two notes, the first note being the note played, and the second being the target note of the bend.

In Example 2, you have a very quick bend followed by a release of the note back to its original pitch. The first note is called a 'grace note' – a note that has no time of its own, but steals a moment of time from the main note. On the notation stave, the target note E is joined to the release note by another bend sign, indicating that this note is not re-picked. On the tab stave, this is indicated by the note being bracketed. The technical term for this short grace note is an 'acciaccatura,' but let's not worry too much about that.

Example 3 is a pre-bend. The note is bent silently and then picked and released so that you only hear the note falling in pitch.

Example 4 is quick bend similar to Example 2, except that the target note for the bend is only one half-step/semitone or one fret higher. As usual the notation stave shows the actual pitches, but in this case the tab stave has a ½ sign above the arrow to indicate a half-step bend.

Example 5 shows a slower one-fret bend.

Example 6 demonstrates unison bends. The fifth fret on the B string is played at the same time as the seventh fret on the G-string, and the G-string note is bent up two frets so that it reaches the same pitch as the B-string note you are already holding.

Vibrato uses a similar technique to bending. It is a rhythmic fluctuation in pitch, usually achieved by pulling the string out of its usual alignment and then returning it again. Try adding vibrato to the note shown above by either pushing it towards the D-string and releasing it or pulling it towards the B-string and releasing it. (I prefer to push a bend and pull vibrato – but experiment and see what works for you.)

LEAD PLAYING

EXERCISE 89, CD TRACK 68 / Bends, vibrato, and triplet runs

1) Slow bends   2) Quick bend followed by release

3) Pre-bend   4) Quick half step bend   5) Slow half-step bend

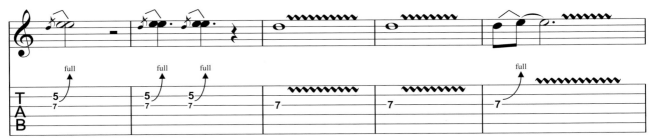

6) Unison bends   7) Slow vibrato 8) Normal vibrato   9) Bend with vibrato

10) Triplet runs   11) Bend/slur combinations

Examples 7 and 8 demonstrate slow and normal vibrato.

Example 9 is a another two-fret bend but this time the bend is held to the end of the bar and vibrato is added. Just allow the bend to release a little and then push it back, moving it to and fro to create the vibrato.

The piece ends with some triplet runs and a characteristic blues bend/pull-off combination. Example 10 shows an example of a triplet run on a minor pentatonic scale, where you play three notes to a beat and use hammer-ons and pull-offs to gain speed and fluency – try copying this idea and making up some runs of your own. Example 11 is a bend-up/let-down/pull-off/hammer-on combination all done with the fret hand. You only need two pick strokes to play the entire figure.

PRO TIP

Practice each example on its own, taking your time to build strength in your fingers. Even with light-gauge strings on your guitar, bending can be tough!

■ THEORY

In some tabs a bend uses the curved line of a slur but has BU (bend up) written above. Similar abbreviations are used for let down (LD), hammer-on (HO) and so on. Perhaps the most obscure is BSS, which means bend slightly sharp.

Before we begin using these new techniques in a solo we are going to take the notes of an A blues scale and play them higher up the neck, in the seventh position. The notes of the scale have not changed at all; we are simply learning to play the same notes in a different position. This extends the range of the scale, which now has a top note of D, and changes the relationships between the notes so that any hammer-on or pull-off techniques can be played differently. Learn the scale shape thoroughly, and then find ways to slide on a string to connect it to shape one.

PRO TIP

I find the quickest way to learn a new scale shape is to use one finger per fret and think of it as a fingering. Starting on the lowest string, this scale would be: 2 4, 1 4, 1 4, 1 2 3, 2 4, 2 4. Does that work for you?

EXERCISE 90 / Blues scale in A, shape two

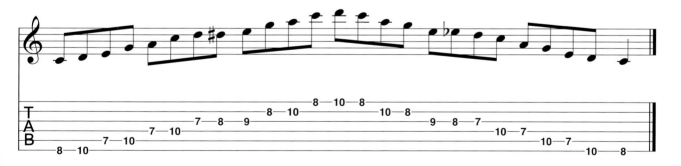

Blues scale shape two

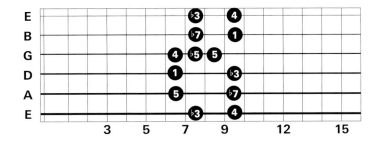

■ THEORY

This shape leaves out the blues scale's flattened fifth on the A string, sixth fret, but only because it doesn't fall under the fingers easily. Try putting it back in with a slide up from frets six to seven.

Exercise 91, 'Jimmy or Jimi?,' combines the two scale shapes we now know and most of the new techniques we looked at in Exercise 89 to create an authentic rock guitar solo. Here's a walk-through of the opening bars to get you started.

The piece begins with a slide 'from nowhere' up to notes that belong to scale shape two. Start around the fifth or sixth fret, pick the note and slide your finger quickly up the string to the ninth fret, applying pressure along the string so that you hear it skid over the frets. Release the pressure when you get to the ninth fret to create the staccato (indicated by the dot over the note).

In the next bar the upward bend is very quick, but the release comes rhythmically on the second eighth-note of the bar, and this short lick ends with some fast vibrato on the D-string. To keep the piece simple all of the bends are 'full' or whole-tone bends – always support the finger that is doing the bend by adding more fingers to the string whenever possible.

Bar three uses the same quick upward bend and slower release to begin an answering phrase that ends in a bend that is then vibratoed. Not an easy technique, but one that's well worth acquiring.

Bar four repeats bar two (question and answer again!) but ends with a rapid hammer-on run leading to a rising phrase with a vibratoed seventh fret D.

The end of bar nine quotes the opening notes again as the beginning of the second section. The first eight bars of rhythm are repeated as the solo stretches out to include higher notes from blues scale shape two. Notice that the material in the opening bars is used as a building block or 'motif' and is often quoted and varied during the course of the piece. Bars three, seven, and 11 are almost identical, and bar 15 very similar. This helps to link the phrases of the solo together so that it makes sense as a piece of music.

LEAD PLAYING

EXERCISE 91, **CD TRACK 69** / 'Jimmy Or Jimi?'

the electric guitar handbook

Exercise 92, the rhythm part to 'Jimmy or Jimi?,' begins with a new chord: E7#9. This great crunchy-sounding chord is closely associated with Jimi Hendrix as he used it often, most notably in the rhythm part of 'Purple Haze.' It is a movable shape and you should try it at other frets too. The rest of the rhythm part to this piece uses just two major bar chord shapes. One is based on the open E major chord, the other on the open A major chord. Once again we have fret-hand muting (notes that are written as XXX); mastering this percussive effect is an important part of rhythm guitar playing. The piece is essentially made from an eight-bar phrase played twice.

PRO TIP

These movable chords are very useful; each one can be played at any fret and when you've mastered them you will be able to play any major chord in at least two positions. To really make use of them you need to learn which note in each shape is the root and know that the chord takes its name from that note. Knowing the names of the notes on the lowest two strings is important here – refer to the complete note guide at the back of the book and practice these two shapes chromatically (fret by fret) saying aloud the name of each chord.

Movable chords for 'Jimmy or Jimi?'

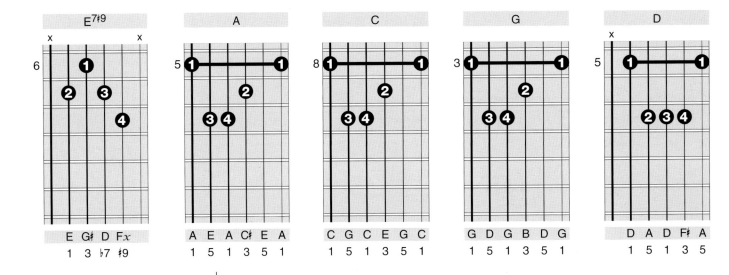

EXERCISE 92 'Jimmy Or Jimi?' rhythm part

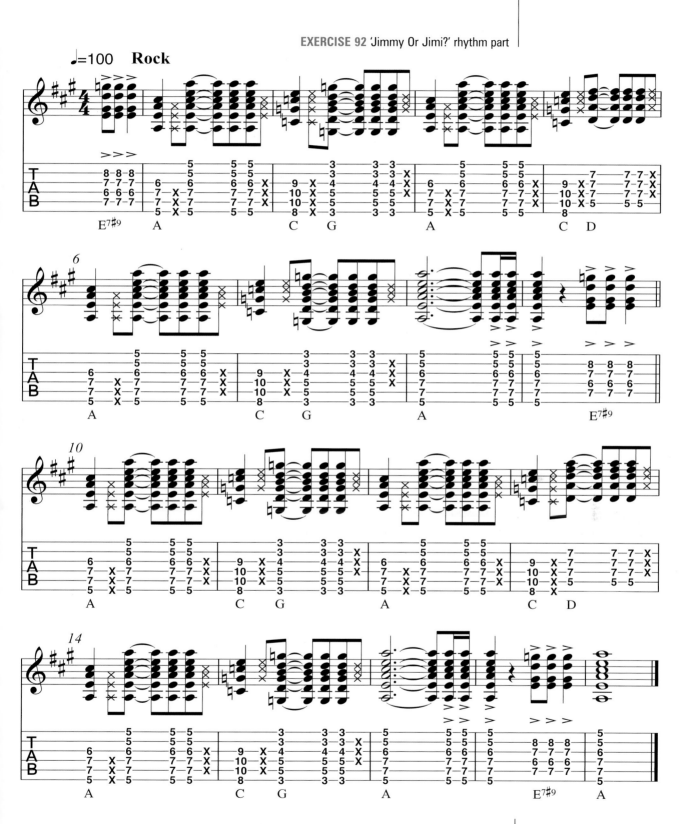

Exercise 93 is a rock'n'roll-style solo that introduces two-note slides using finger one and finger three. It begins with a characteristic riff that was made famous by Chuck Berry but which can be used in blues and rock styles. Notice the grace notes in the notation part, which tell you that the slide is performed very quickly, 'stealing' its time from the main note. Many of the notes in this piece come from arpeggios of the chords rather than from the blues scale; much of it has a 'major' flavor rather than the blues scale minor flavor.

Watch out for bar 10, which has another Chuck-inspired riff; this time it's a unison bend where the bent note and held note are played separately. Start by picking and bending the seventh-fret G-string. Hold the bend while you also pick the fifth-fret B-string two times. Let the two notes blend together.

The lead guitar is unaccompanied in this track so that you can clearly hear what's going on. The underlying feel here and in rock'n'roll generally is straight rather than shuffle, as this seems better suited to the faster tempos. Even though Chuck Berry started in the 50s, his songs are still popular with guitarists today – check out his playing on 'Johnny B. Goode.'

LEAD PLAYING

EXERCISE 93, CD TRACK 70 / Rock'n'roll Chuck-style

Blues scales are not only used for wailing lead guitar solos. They are also great for riffs and rhythm parts. Exercise 94 is inspired by guitarists like Joe Satriani ('Satch Boogie') and Eddie Van Halen ('Hot For Teacher'). It uses a blues scale, an A5 chord, triplet and open-string pull-offs, and blues-scale double-stops to create a flowing, uptempo introduction to a verse or song. Watch out for the staccato Cs on the second beat in most bars – release the finger pressure as soon as you've played this note. The triplets should be played using fingers three, two, and one in the blues scale shape one position. Put the three fingers down together and only pick the first note of the triplet, pulling off the fingers in succession.

The last three or four pieces in this section represent a thorough study of the basic techniques of lead guitar playing. In places these pieces are challenging, and I strongly recommend that you keep returning to any difficult sections, practicing them slowly and accurately. Listen closely to the recorded versions on CD, and do your best to copy not just the notes, but also the style, phrasing, and possibly even the sound of the tracks. It can take time to build technique, so be patient and persevere.

In the next section we will continue to study lead guitar, but now moving beyond the notes of the blues scale.

LEAD PLAYING

EXERCISE 94, CD TRACK 71 / 'Joe Meets Eddie'

the electric guitar handbook

beyond the blues scale

The arpeggios we have played so far have mostly been of the chiming 'let ring' variety, used in place of strumming as a textural accompaniment. Arpeggios can have a great deal of melodic value, and sound cool and sophisticated when used for making up riffs and solos.

On the opposite page are two arpeggio 'shapes' shown in a similar way to the blues scale shapes that we have learned. An A7 arpeggio will sound good played over an A7 chord, and a D7 arpeggio will fit a D7 chord. Like blues scale shapes these shapes are movable and can be played starting at any fret. Try playing them both two frets lower; this will give you G7 and C7 arpeggios, which you could use to play over CD track 48 (Exercise 61) which used the chords G7, C7, A7, and D7. See if you can make up a lead guitar part to go with that rhythm part.

EXERCISE 95 / Arpeggios of A7 and D7

A7 arpeggio shape

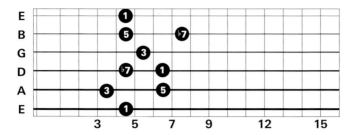

D7 arpeggio shape

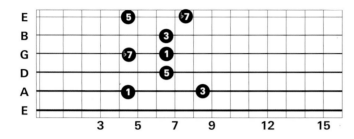

Let's go back to CD track 63 (Exercise 81) to hear how arpeggios can be used to create a rock'n'roll-style riff. The lead part (Exercise 96) is built around a two-bar pattern with a root-note and chord combination followed by a single-note run. All the notes of the single-note run come from the arpeggio of the underlying chord, and the open string chord shapes should be familiar from Part One. Notice the slide 'from nowhere' up to the first note of the run; pick the note two or three frets below your target note and slide up quickly.

EXERCISE 96, CD TRACK 63 / 'Steady As A Rock' lead part

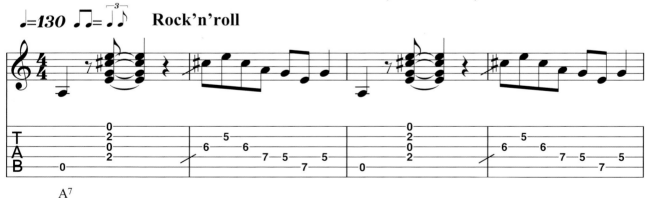

continued over page

the electric guitar handbook

LEAD PLAYING

EXERCISE 96 *continued*

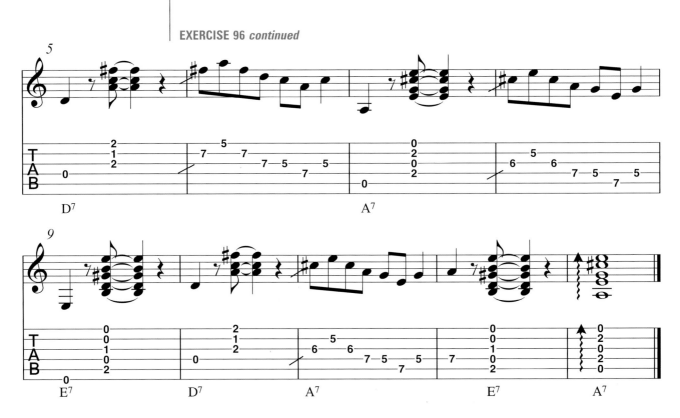

We looked at major pentatonic scales back in Part One, and found they had a bright, twangy quality which contrasted with the blues scale's dark bluesy quality. Major pentatonic scales can be movable just like blues scales, and here we have two movable scale shapes in the key of C major and two in G major. An important difference between the blues scale and the major pentatonic scale is that you can use the blues scale to play over all the chords in a blues or in most rock chord sequences. You don't have to change key as the chords change. The major pentatonic, however, is best played over its own major chord; that's not to say it can't be played over other chords, but some notes will need careful handling if, for example, you play a C major pentatonic scale over a G major chord.

the electric guitar handbook

EXERCISE 97, C & G movable major pentatonic scales

C major pentatonic (A minor pentatonic Shape 1)

C major pentatonic (A minor pentatonic Shape 2)

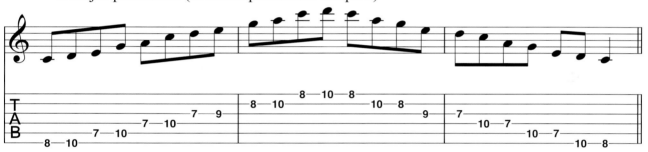

G major pentatonic with slide to 5th position

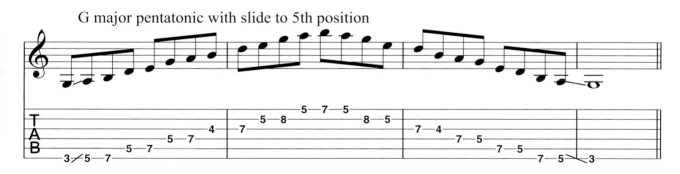

G major pentatonic in 7th position

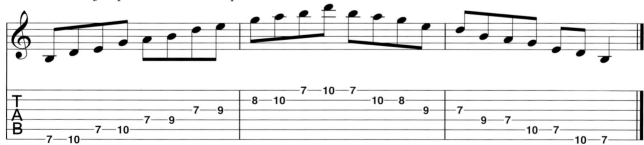

C major pentatonic scales

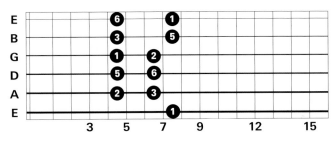

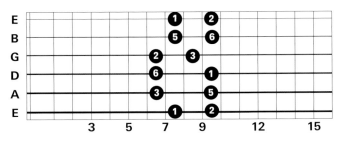

G major pentatonic scales

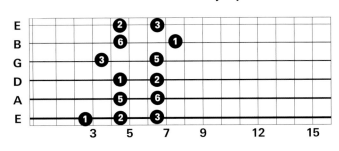

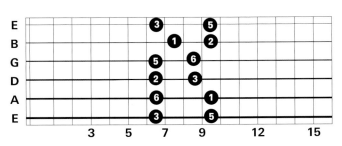

So does that mean that you need to learn loads of major pentatonic scale shapes as well as blues scales? No! If you take a close look at the two C major pentatonic scale shapes you will find they are exactly the same as the A minor pentatonic scale shapes we already know. Both scales have the same five notes, but a different note is the root. As we change the note that is the root, the relationships between the other notes of the scale change also, and the minor intervals of the minor pentatonic are replaced by the major intervals of the major pentatonic.

EXERCISE 98 / A minor and C major pentatonic scales

A minor pentatonic:

| A | C | D | E | G | A |
| Root | Minor 3rd | Perfect 4th | Perfect 5th | Minor 7th | Root |

2 C major pentatonic:

| C | D | E | G | A | C |
| Root | Major 2nd | Major 3rd | Perfect 5th | Major 6th | Root |

Exercise 99, 'Twang Thang,' uses our two new pentatonic scales in a characteristically twangy country-style piece. Notice the slides that connect the two scale shapes

EXERCISE 99, CD TRACK 72 / 'Twang Thang' lead part

PRO TIP

See if you can work out the thirds and sixths in other common keys.

together, and the 'major' flavored bend-and-release in bars two and four. Always aim to bend to a specific pitch – don't just heave the string vaguely across the neck as it will just make you sound out of tune. The staccatos may well require careful attention but they are an important part of the style.

From bar nine the piece uses an approach based on thirds rather than strictly pentatonic scales. Thirds, and their opposites, sixths, can also have a 'major' sound and are commonly used in music of this style. Use finger one in a 'half barre' when you have two notes at the same fret, and fingers two and three for the notes on adjacent frets. The rhythm part to this piece was first heard on CD track 47, and could be used as a backing track to practice both this solo and one that you make up.

■ THEORY

Some of these thirds are major, some are minor. Can you work out which is which?

As we saw in Exercise 99, thirds can be very useful for creating melodic phrases and connecting runs. Exercise 100 begins with thirds in the key of C major, played first of all on the second and third strings and then on the first and second strings. Compare these fingerings with those used in Exercise 99.

If you imagine a third played upside down, with the lower note moved up an octave, you would have a sixth. In other words, C to E is a third, but E to C is a sixth. The second part of Exercise 100 shows sixths in the key of C major, again played on

EXERCISE 100 / Thirds and sixths in C major

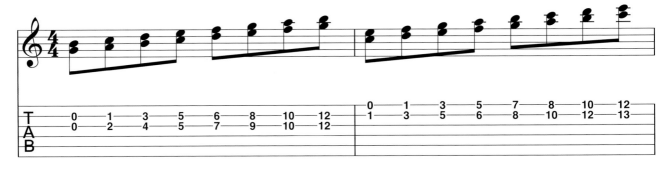

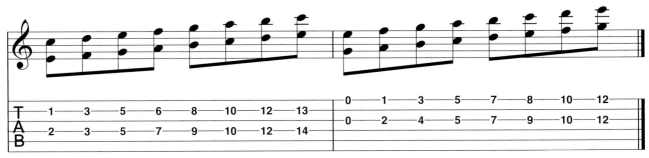

two different pairs of strings. Notice how the two intervals have a similar flavor, and experiment with them using CD track 47 as a backing track.

We have tended to focus on pentatonic scales, and their close relative the blues scale, because they are the most common scales used by electric guitar players. We have also mentioned major scales, which are seven note scales, but have used them mainly in explaining keys, chords, and intervals. In Exercise 101 we are looking at a different kind of seven-note scale, in the key of F-sharp minor. Try playing this scale smoothly and legato, and watch out for the extended position covering five frets on the D-string.

■ THEORY

Each major scale has a 'relative minor,' a minor scale that shares the same key signature and is made up of the same seven notes. If you look at the key signature for the F-sharp minor scale you will see three sharps, the same as for A major. Simply by starting on a different note of the A major scale, we have created a new scale. There are several types of minor scale, and this one is known as the 'natural minor.' One way to describe this scale would be to say that it is a major scale played with the sixth note of the scale as the root. The study of modes is beyond the scope of this book, but you might like to know that the natural minor is sometimes known as the Aeolian mode.

EXERCISE 101 / F-sharp minor scale

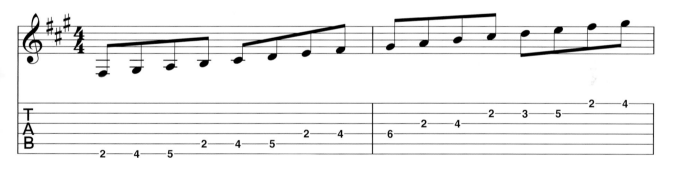

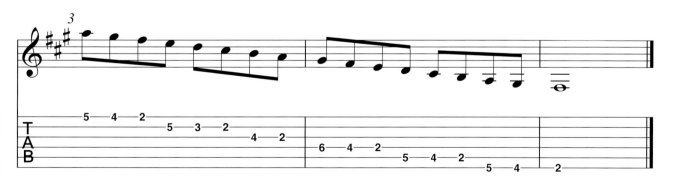

the electric guitar handbook

LEAD PLAYING

PRO TIP

Notice how the backing track begins sparsely, with just a few accents in each bar, before rocking out for the repeat. This is a great way of adding interest to a repeated section.

Exercise 102 uses the F-sharp minor scale to create a flowing and suitably dark-sounding metal-style song intro. It is played using just downstrokes for added emphasis, and you should aim to make it completely legato. When you've mastered it, try adding some palm muting – it can be very effective on riffs like these. Minor scales seem to suit the 'dark' flavors preferred by metal bands. We'll look at another possible use for this scale in the next exercise.

EXERCISE 102, CD TRACK 73 / F-sharp minor metal riffs

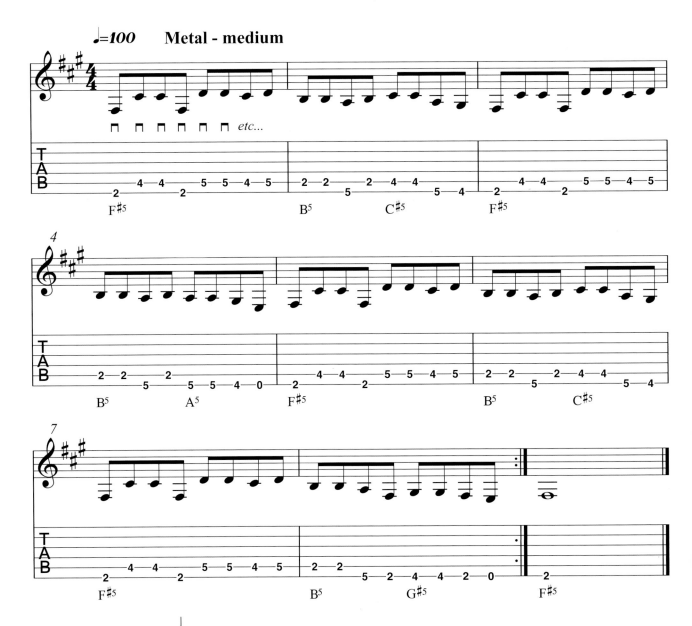

This section is titled 'Beyond the blues scale' but we need to return to blues scales to look at a possible use of the natural minor scale. Exercise 103 begins with the blues scale arranged up the guitar using only the sixth string. Then we have the blues scale played using 5 chords, where each note of the scale is used as the root of a chord. The exercise uses the two-note 5 chord but you could try it using the heavier sounding three-note version too.

EXERCISE 103 / Blues scale in 5 chords

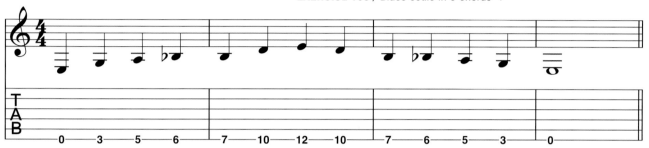

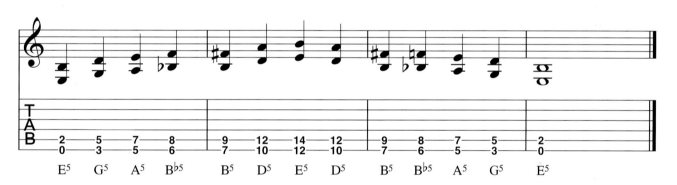

Two- and three-note 5 chords

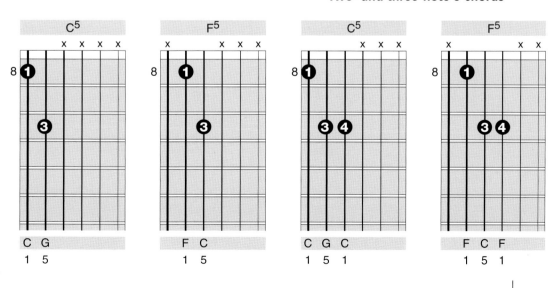

LEAD PLAYING

In Exercise 101 we learned the F-sharp minor scale played on the guitar in the second position. Exercise 104 begins with the same scale transposed to the key of E, arranged using only the E-string as above. The second part of the exercise shows the same scale played using 5 chords – practice these shapes until you are used to sliding them around the guitar.

PRO TIP

Remember not to stare fixedly at your fret hand while you play. You will hit the correct fret more often if you look where your hand should be going to – in other words, if you must look at all, look ahead to the target!

EXERCISE 104 / E minor scale on sixth string

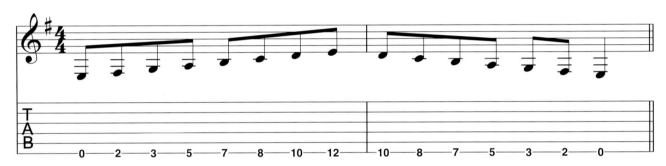

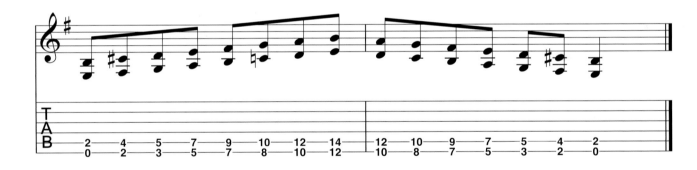

EXERCISE 105, CD TRACK 74 / Metal riffs in E minor

the electric guitar handbook

If you have played the blues scale and the natural minor scale in 5 chords, it's time we tried using them both together, in this case to grind out some serious metal riffs. In Exercise 105 (previous page) you will find notes from both scales , showing that it's OK to switch from one to the other. In fact, all the blues-scale notes are contained in the natural minor except one – the diminished fifth, which can have a very dissonant sound and is a good one to emphasise in this style of music. Remember that the rests (the silences) are an important ingredient and you will need to mute (or 'damp') the strings very accurately. You could try using your pick hand to mute the strings after playing an open string, but using your fret hand to mute the strings after a fretted chord.

There is a similarity between this piece and Exercise 78 (CD track 60) which also used 5 chords slid around the guitar, but using drop D tuning. Try tuning to drop D and playing Exercise 105 using the one-finger five chord shape that we used in Exercise 78; if you read the lowest note of the tab as the root note of each chord you will be playing in D minor and should be rewarded by hearing some powerful modern metal sounds if you use some distortion. These 5 chords are not limited to metal, however, and can be used in many other styles.

To end our section on 'beyond the blues scale' we are going to return to the subject of arpeggios, because they sound great and have an incredible number of uses in a wide range of styles. The rhythm track to Exercise 106 can be found in Exercise 72 (CD track 56) so be sure to try this lead guitar part both with the backing band and with another guitar player if possible.

The arpeggios in the first two bars are based on the familiar open-string chord shapes we learned back in Part Two, Section One. The following two bars use shapes based on the movable triads we looked at in Part Two, Section Four. These first four bars are repeated with a slight variation in bar eight, before moving on, in bar nine, to a section which is again based on movable triad shapes. The chord symbols in brackets identify the altered chords being played (Dadd9 and Asus4), while the other chord symbols refer to the chords from the rhythm part.

This track is fairly fast and will test your picking and fretting techniques, and the coordination between them. Break it down into smaller sections for practicing, and do your homework by checking out what notes you are playing and which chord they come from. If you do the job thoroughly you'll be able to make up your own guitar parts using a similar approach.

In this section we have looked at lead guitar parts that go beyond the blues scale. We have used arpeggios, major pentatonics, minor scales, and thirds and sixths to create riffs, licks, and solos in styles from metal to country. Something that you should take from this is that music sounds the way it does because of the notes that are played, as well as because of the way they are played. If any of the styles covered here appeal to you, you'll need to go deeper to find out more about the note choices you need to make to get them to sound right. In the next section we are going to look at some advanced techniques for soloing.

EXERCISE 106, CD TRACK 75 / 'Fives And Nines' lead part

advanced soloing techniques

In this section we are going to look at some of the more unusual sounds that guitar players create as special effects.

At certain frets on the guitar there are strange bell-like sounds that are played without holding down the string. They are known as natural harmonics and are a phenomenon common to all stringed instruments. To sound a harmonic cleanly, you have to position your fret hand finger directly over the fret, rather than in its normal place, which is just behind the fret.

Twelfth-fret harmonics are the easiest to produce so we will start with these. Do not hold the string down – just touch it lightly, and pluck the string near the bridge. Work your way across the 12th fret from the low E-string to the high E-string and you should hear something like the first six sounds on the CD track. Now play all six strings in turn at the seventh fret, the fifth fret and finally the fourth fret. You have to position your fret hand finger very accurately to get the higher harmonics to pop out clearly. I prefer to lay one finger across the string as if doing a barre, but other players use the tips of their fingers. You need to release your finger from the string immediately after picking to get the note to ring on. The CD track ends with a harmonics-based run using seventh and 12th fret harmonics which is played slowly at first, using eighth-notes, and then at twice the speed, using 16th-notes. Notice the vibrato in bar 11, which was performed using the 'whammy bar' or 'tremolo arm.' More on this later!

■ THEORY

Notice in Exercise 107 the different ways in which harmonics are notated. On the notation stave the actual pitch of the harmonic is written accurately, but a diamond shaped note is used. As harmonics are very high in pitch, we use the sign '8va...' to signify that the notes are an octave higher than written. On the tab stave there is no attempt to notate the actual pitch; instead, the fret number is written with the sign 'Harm...' above.

ADVANCED SOLOING TECHNIQUES

PRO TIP

Harmonics can be made to pop out more easily if you have some distortion running. Many harmonics can be found in more than one place. For example, the fourth fret harmonics can also be found at the ninth fret, 16th fret and somewhere around your front pickup. There are also weaker harmonics found in front of and behind the third fret, and over the second fret. If you run your finger slowly along the sixth string while picking rapidly near the bridge you should be able to hear all sorts of random harmonic squeals.

EXERCISE 107, **CD TRACK 76** / Natural harmonics

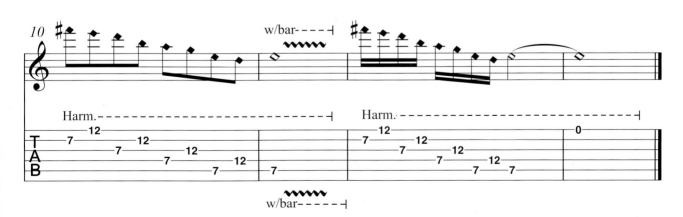

the electric guitar handbook

Harmonics are available on fretted notes too, but you need to use your right-hand to sound them. If you're holding a note at the third fret, all the harmonics we played in Exercise 107 will be found three frets higher than before, at the 15th, tenth, eighth and seventh frets. Try holding down the sixth string at the third fret and touching the harmonic point at the 15th fret with the index finger of your picking hand. Now pick the string, with the pick held between your thumb and middle finger. This is called an artificial harmonic and is usually marked in the music as 'A.H.'

Electric guitar players have another option, which is to tap the string at the harmonic point with the index finger. These are known as tapped harmonics. Here's how it works. In Exercise 108, we are holding down the G bar chord at the third fret and tapping harmonics around the 15th, tenth and eighth frets; in other words, 12 frets, seven frets and five frets higher than the chord. You could try holding the pick between your thumb and middle finger and tapping with your index finger, or holding the pick in the normal way and tapping with your middle finger. Notes that are tapped have a capital T written above them. You will sometimes see tapped notes notated in other ways including circles or squares around notes; written instructions are also

EXERCISE 108, CD TRACK 77 / Artificial and tapped harmonics

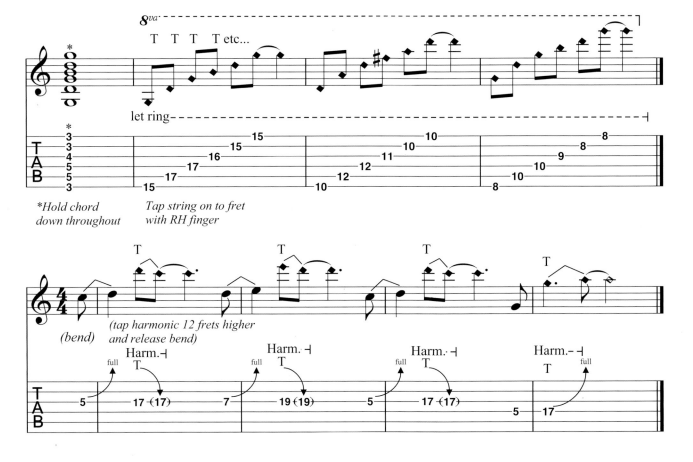

Hold chord down throughout

Tap string on to fret with RH finger

common in tablature. The way that tricks and effects like these are written varies between different editions, but there should usually be a key to explain what's what.

The second half of Exercise 108 is a phrase that combines bent notes with tapped harmonics. Play the third string, fifth fret, then bend the string and hold the bend; tap the harmonic 12 frets up (at the 17th fret) and release the bend. Continue bending, tapping, and releasing as instructed in the tab, except for the note in the last bar, which is bent after being tapped as a harmonic. These notes come from the A blues scale, but the tapped harmonics give the phrase a very modern twist.

If you can tap a harmonic, it figures that you can tap and hold any string against the fret and it could sound just like you picked it. Many guitarists have used pull-offs between fretted notes and open strings but a certain Eddie Van Halen was the first to get his right hand in on the act and play some jaw-droppingly fast arpeggios using combinations of tapped pick hand notes and fret-hand hammer-ons and pull-offs. If you don't include open strings you could have a pattern that can be moved around the neck. 'Two-hand tapping' has now become a standard and accepted way of playing both electric and acoustic guitar.

EXERCISE 109, **CD TRACK 78** / Two-hand tapping

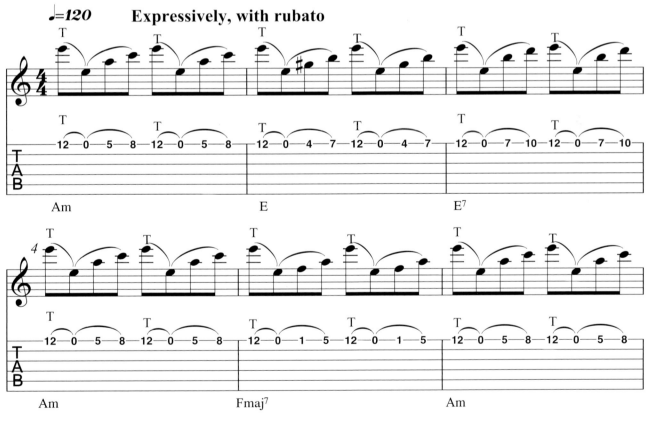

continued over page

the electric guitar handbook

LEAD PLAYING

EXERCISE 109 *continued*

Faster

The best way to get started in this style of playing is to work out the notes of an arpeggio on just one string. The example begins with an A minor arpeggio (the notes A, C and E,) beginning with a tap on the 12th fret with the picking hand which also pulls off on to the open string. The fretting hand then hammers on at the fifth fret with finger one and the eighth with finger four. Tap once more at the 12th fret and the riff begins again.

Exercise 109 is based on chords of A minor, E major, F major seventh and G-sharp diminished, using the open E string as a pedal. On the CD the music is played twice, firstly at a slow speed that allows you to hear the detail, and then at a faster speed, which gives you an idea of what's possible. Muting the unused open strings is always a problem in this style of playing. If you listen closely to the CD track you can hear the lower strings sounding as the track progresses; this is caused by 'sympathetic vibration,' where the repeated playing of the open E has gradually set the other strings ringing.

On the faster section I muted the lowest strings with the heel of my picking hand; see if you can do likewise!

■ THEORY

Rubato is an Italian word that means 'stolen.' Slight variations in the pulse of the music work well in slower pieces; it's as if you 'steal' some time from one note and then pay it back by lengthening another.

PRO TIP
Eddie Van Halen used his index finger for tapping and always held his pick between his thumb and middle finger. If you are used to holding the pick between thumb and index finger, try tapping and pulling off with the middle finger.

Arpeggios can go upwards, downwards, forwards and back on themselves, and Exercise 110 gives some examples using the first bar of Exercise 109.

The first example (bars one and two) begins with a tap at the 12th fret, which is pulled off on to the eighth fret (use finger four) and then the fifth fret (finger one). The open string is then sounded by pulling off the first finger, thus creating a descending arpeggio.

The second example (bars three and four) uses triplet eighth-notes and begins with a tap at the 12th fret and pull-off on to the open string. The remaining notes of the six-note pattern are all sounded with the fret hand.

The third example (bars five and six) takes this idea even further, with the first note of the bar sounded by tapping with the pick hand, and all the remaining notes of the bar played by hammering on or pulling off with the fret hand.

Try them out and then see if you can make up some examples of your own.

the electric guitar handbook

LEAD PLAYING

EXERCISE 110 / Variations on Exercise 109

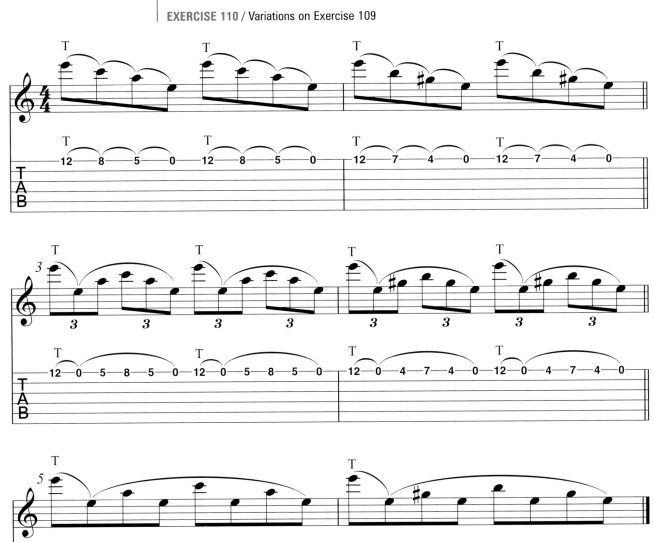

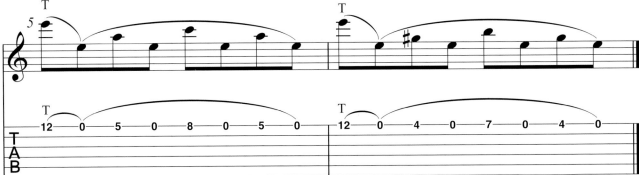

We have found that it is possible to tap notes with the pick hand, and it shouldn't be too difficult to tap notes with the fret hand as well. In fact, you can tap two or more notes at once, leading some guitarists to develop a whole new style of guitar playing based on chordal tapping with the fret hand while adding melodies with the pick hand.

In Exercise 111 we are tapping chord shapes as arpeggios using the first two fingers of both hands. The fret hand fingers tap the notes on the G and A strings and the pick hand fingers tap the notes on the B and D strings. Use your neck hand coming over the top of the neck rather than the usual position, which should allow you to use the outside of your hand to damp the open strings. You can 'palm' the pick while doing this, holding it between the curled pick-hand fingers that you are not using. Alternatively, some players put it between their teeth – see which works best for you.

EXERCISE 111, CD TRACK 79 / Chordal tapping

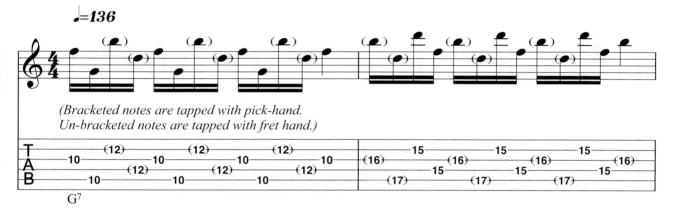

(Bracketed notes are tapped with pick-hand.
Un-bracketed notes are tapped with fret hand.)

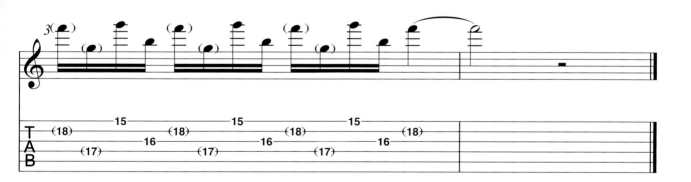

Exercise 112 goes deeper into the world of two-hand tapping, showing that it is possible to cross from string to string while tapping. Essentially it's a four-note minor arpeggio with the open string as its root. By moving the middle two notes up a whole step (two frets) you then get a major arpeggio with the fifth-fret note as its root. Tap

the electric guitar handbook

Chord shapes for two-handed tapping

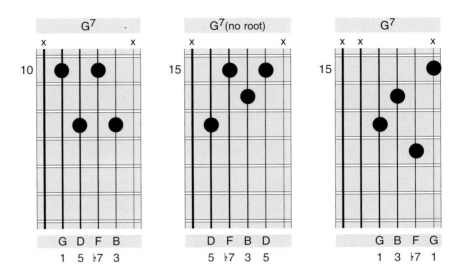

and pull-off with your right hand index or middle finger on the note at the 12th fret; all the other notes are hammered on or pulled off with the left hand. As you can see, you can play it on any string you like! It will require a lot of co-ordination between the 'tapping' hand and the 'hammer-on and pull-off' hand to get it fast and smooth, and you need to be able to stretch your fret hand from the third fret to the seventh fret. Take it slowly at first, relax, and don't struggle!

This example ends with a lick that shows how you can also use your right hand to add notes to fast runs. This one looks a bit like a blues scale but is really a finger pattern using a 12th-fret tap and fingers four, three, and one pulling off all the way across the guitar.

Check out Van Halen's 'Eruption' or 'Hot For Teacher' for more examples of this style of playing.

THE VIBRATO BAR

Leo Fender's marketing people have a lot to answer for, because they described the Fender Stratocaster's bridge as having a 'tremolo' device. In fact, tremolo is a regular fluctuation in volume, not pitch, and so it should really be called a 'vibrato' bar or arm. However, what we are about to get up to here hardly comes under the heading of vibrato – perhaps the 80s term 'whammy bar' would be more appropriate. Many guitars today are supplied with vibrato bridges, but unless you have a Floyd Rose or a Wilkinson or something similar you may be in for some tuning problems after each bout of whammy abuse.

Exercise 113 begins with a trick which I call 'picking with the bar,' a technique where dipping the bar seems to feed energy into the string. Pick a note, then dip and release the bar, sliding the fret-hand finger up two frets. Co-ordinate the dipping and releasing of the bar with each new note you slide to. This use of the bar is often called

EXERCISE 112, CD TRACK 80 / Van Halen tapping

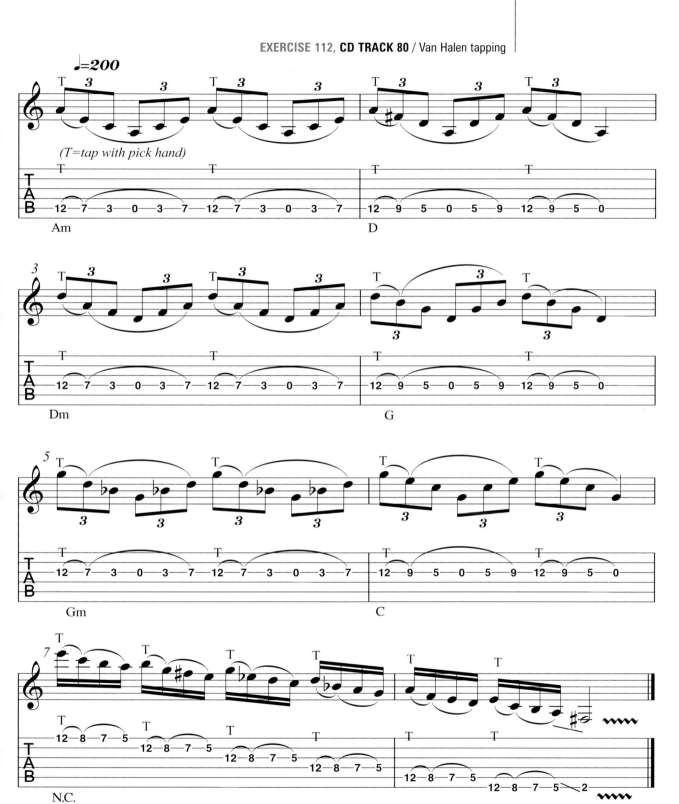

(T=tap with pick hand)

the electric guitar handbook

LEAD PLAYING

a 'scoop.' You only pick the first note of the phrase, so it's like using the bar instead of the pick. Vibrato the last note with the bar – notice that is has a different quality to finger vibrato.

The second part of the exercise gets you using your ear to dip the bar in tune. It begins with a fret-hand tap and pull-off on the fifth fret of the low E-string. That's the note A followed by the open E. Then you dip the bar all the way down until the open E-string reaches the note A an octave down from where you began. Hold the bar down and tap again at the fifth fret, releasing the bar slowly; you will hear the note climb all the way back up to the A you started on. If you listen closely you should be able to get these notes in tune. Try to hold the target pitch in your head as you dip the bar – it's OK to over-bend the note slightly and let the bar up to find the note as I do on the CD track.

The example ends with some characteristic squealing harmonics played over the fourth fret on the top two strings, which are dipped and vibratoed with the bar.

In this section we have looked at natural and artificial harmonics, two-hand tapping, and whammy bar tricks. As well as Eddie Van Halen, you should check out Joe Satriani and Steve Vai if this is your kind of playing.

EXERCISE 113, CD TRACK 81 / Whammy bar tricks

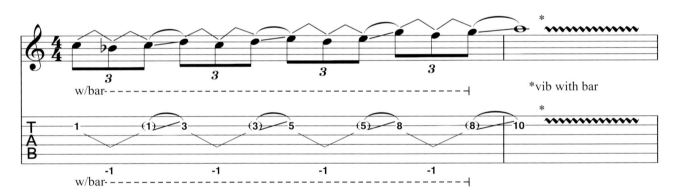

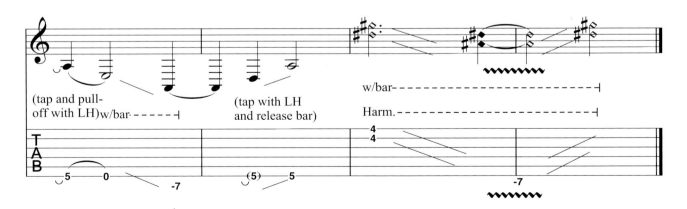

■ moving on up

Exercise 114 uses some of the three-note chord shapes below, with the addition of pedal notes in the bass and occasional arpeggios. This is a fully fleshed-out and complex guitar part and you may need to work at fretting and strumming these chords accurately. You will be changing the shape several times in some bars. If you find it difficult, practice each bar in turn, slowly at first, and look for fingers that can stay on the same string and slide to the next position. Sometimes you won't need to lift a finger at all between two chords. If you can, keep it down! These chords are harmonically complex and rich; distortion will turn that complexity into mush, so use a clean sound.

PRO TIP

A simple trick used by many guitarists playing in this style is to add a capo. Try playing this exercise with a capo on the second fret. It not only shifts the pitch up a whole step/tone but also seems to make the texture a little thinner, giving the track a brighter, lighter flavor.

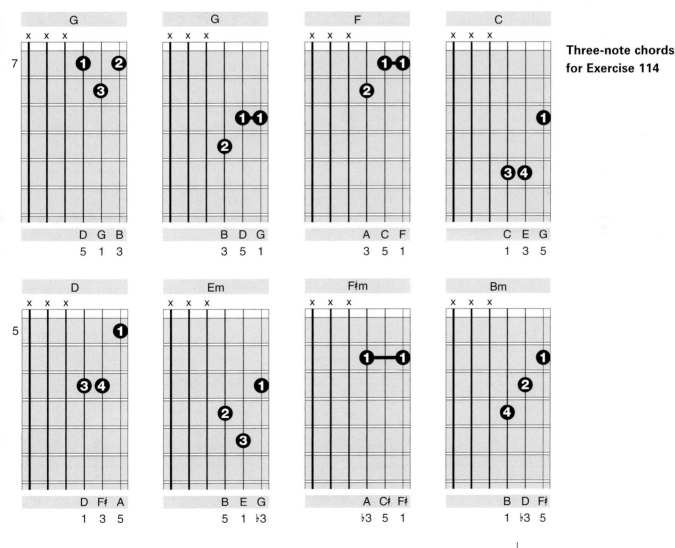

Three-note chords for Exercise 114

LEAD PLAYING

EXERCISE 114, CD TRACK 82 / Arpeggios and bar chords with pedals

We touched on triads at the end of part two, and as we are looking to be more adventurous moving around the neck, it makes sense to return to them at this point. The first three diagrams below are inversions of a C major triad played on the second, third and fourth strings. Then we have C major triads on the top three strings. As these are movable shapes (with one exception) they can be played at any fret – work out which note is the root note and it will give you the name of the chord.

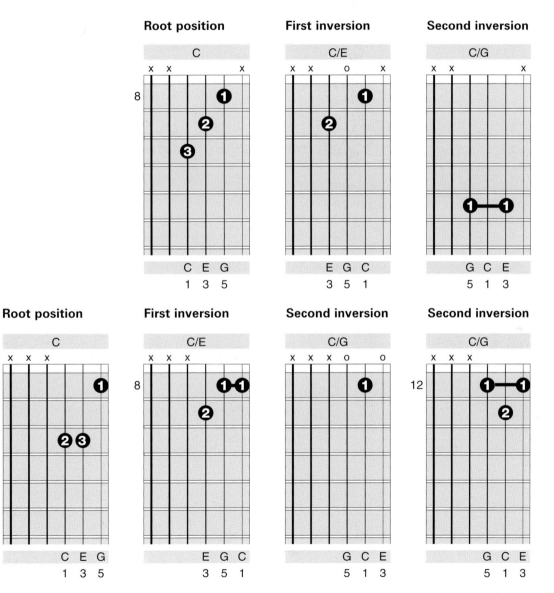

the electric guitar handbook

LEAD PLAYING

EXERCISE 115, CD TRACK 83 / Triads with pedal notes

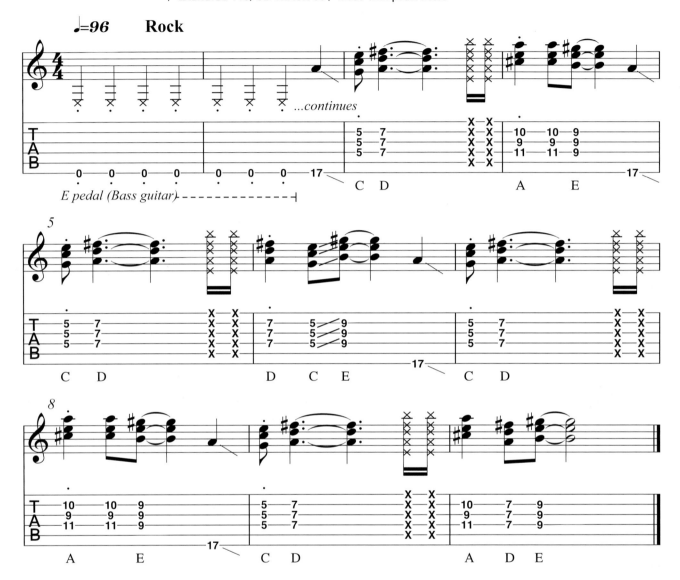

Exercise 115 mainly uses the second inversion shape – a very useful shape, as it can be played with just one finger, which is slid around the guitar at the fifth, seventh, and ninth frets. There are occasional muted notes and a long glissando from the 17th fret. Whizz your finger down the string, pressing lightly, releasing the pressure around the fifth fret. Notice the one-note bassline – it's all played over an E pedal in the bass.

■ **THEORY**

A glissando is also known as a slide.

the electric guitar handbook

Adding one finger to the second inversion triad shape on the D, G and B strings creates a movable sus4 chord. Exercise 116 is an example of a rhythm part built on alternating major and sus4 chords. There is no bass part this time; the pedal note comes from the guitar's own open E string, played 'in the gaps.' Notice how the rhythm is 'pushed,' coming in before the first beat but returning to the downbeat half way through. This sort of rhythmic shift adds drive and lets you play the riff twice

EXERCISE 116, CD TRACK 84 / Triads, sus4 chords, and E pedal

the electric guitar handbook

EXERCISE 117, **CD TRACK 85** / 'Dr Punkenstein'

without sounding repetitive. Don't overdo the distortion on a track like this – too much and these triads will sound mushy.

Exercise 117, 'Dr Punkenstein,' mixes up open-string chords, single-note riffs, and movable 5 chords in the style of the classic punk-rock bands. We start with a crashing E chord and fast alternate picking on the bass strings. Crank up the distortion a little, as you're looking for the punk buzz-saw guitar sound. You will probably get best results off the bridge pickup. You can figure out the A5 and B5 chord shapes from the tab – notice that we are using the three-note 5 chord which doubles the root note an octave higher. This adds power and thickness to the sound but has a downside in that the shape is harder to slide around than the more straightforward two-note 5 chord. The fast tempo may cause some problems too, so practice slowly at first if you need to.

PRO TIP
Experiment with the two-note or three-note 5 chords in your own music and get used to choosing the most appropriate type. Two-note chords are clearer and easier for fast riffing; three-note chords sound bigger and more powerful.

Exercise 118 (next page) is a Motown-inspired rhythm guitar part that features staccato chords played with downstrokes on beats two and four. These movable four-string shapes are very useful for rhythm playing as they make a compact and punchy sound and do not clutter up the lower end of the track. Notice the way the guitar part fits with the snare drum; aim to lock your groove with the backbeat. Playing short staccato rhythms also helps this part to stay clear of the sustained keyboard part.

At bar ten the rhythm intensifies for the middle section and the guitar plays on the quarter-notes before returning to beats two and four from bar 14 to the end. You need

Movable four-string chords

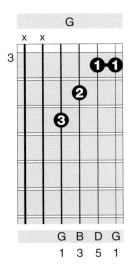
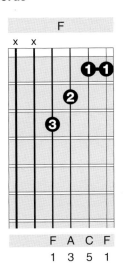
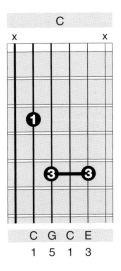

EXERCISE 118, **CD TRACK 86** / Motown-style rhythm part

a clean sound for this type of rhythm part – this was played on a Strat using the bridge pickup with no added effects.

PRO TIP

Guitar players spend far more time playing rhythm than playing lead, so it's probably more important to be a good rhythm player. Make sure that practicing rhythm playing is part of your routine.

At the end of Part Three you should be growing in confidence as both a rhythm and lead guitar player. Hopefully, you are beginning to make up your own solos and riffs using blues scales, major pentatonics, or other scales as appropriate. You should be able to choose chord shapes for your rhythm parts according to the needs of the music you are playing. Be sure to practice playing rhythm as well as lead, and try playing with the click from a metronome to improve your sense of time. Recording your own backing tracks and soloing over them is a great way to improve your all-round ability. Listen closely to your favourite bands' recordings, and try to work out what the guitar players are doing; it may seem difficult at first, but this is the best way to improve your ear and your understanding of what it means to be a guitarist.

In Part Four, we will look at the role of the guitar player in a range of different styles.

the electric guitar handbook

Part 4

- **Putting it all together**
- **Funk**
- **Metal**
- **Indie**
- **Harmony guitars**

■ putting it all together

Part Four brings together the work that we have done on rhythm and lead guitar with a series of more advanced pieces in a range of different styles.

In Exercise 119 (over the page) we are going to return to the blues, and learn a rhythm part and lead part in the key of C.

We have already learned the blues vamp in A major, based around the fifth fret. Moving up to C Major at the eighth fret shouldn't be a problem; using movable shapes you can now play in any key. Notice that in this arrangement of the 12-bar blues we go to chord IV (F major) in the second bar. This is not uncommon, and if you listen to a range of 12-bar blues songs you will hear that some take the IV chord in the second bar and some stay on chord I.

Now take a close look at the first bar. As usual, we are alternating between C5 and C6, with the chord symbol at the bottom of the stave giving the underlying harmony of C. In the past we have always played each chord twice, but here we are playing the C6 chord just once before returning to C5. This is one of many possible variations on the two-note blues vamp pattern.

At the start of the second 12 bars (the second chorus) the band stop playing except for the first beat of each bar, while the lead guitar carries on soloing. We usually call this 'stops' or 'breaks' and it can be a very exciting effect. So if someone you're playing with shouts 'break' when coming to the end of a chorus, you will know what to do! In this chorus we play the F vamp high up at the eighth fret and also low down at the first fret. Watch out for the ending, where a single-note run leads to a chromatic approach to the final chord.

In Exercise 121 we will learn the lead guitar part. On the CD, the lead guitar is panned left and the rhythm guitar panned right so you can play along to both elements. Listen closely to the track and see if you can copy the sound of the palm-muting.

PUTTING IT ALL TOGETHER

EXERCISE 119, CD TRACK 87 / Blues in C, rhythm part

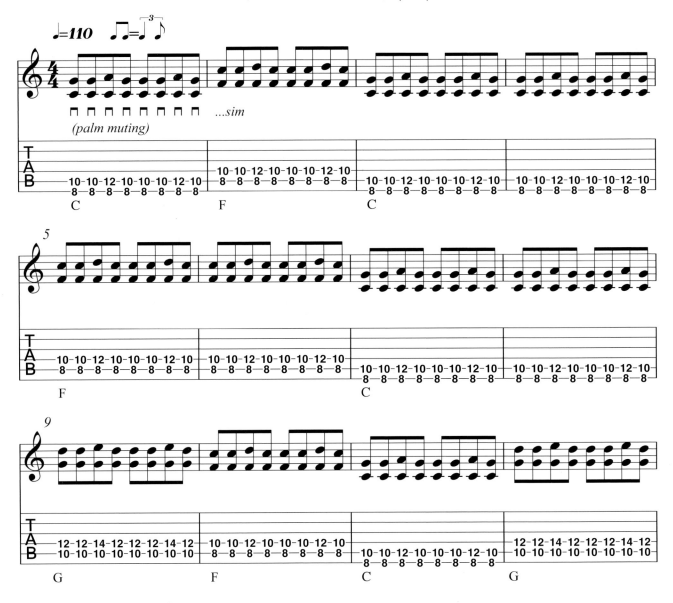

EXERCISE 119 *continued*

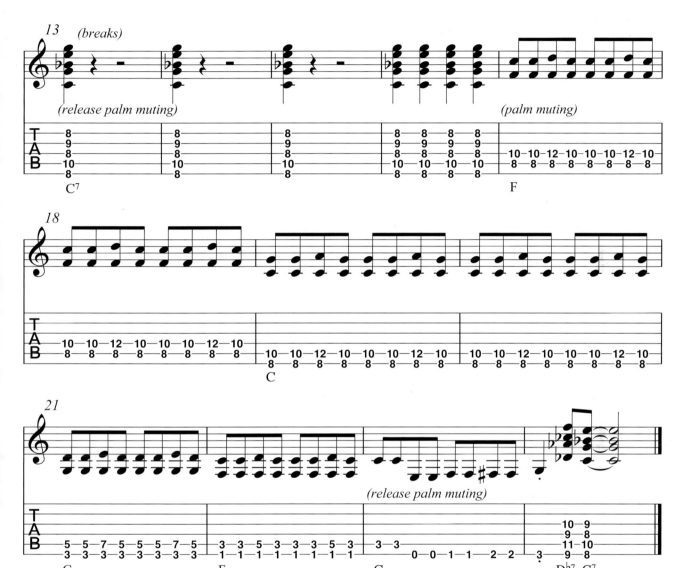

PUTTING IT ALL TOGETHER

EXERCISE 120 / Blues scales in C

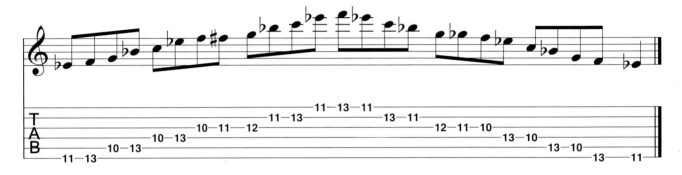

PRO TIP

Check that you're using alternate picking when you play these scales.

The lead guitar part to CD track 87 is based on the two movable blues scale shapes that we learned in Part Three, Section One. Back then, we were in the key of A, so now that we have moved to C, here are the same two scales in the new key.

Play them both, and as you learn Exercise 121 refer back to the scales so that you can see where the notes of the solo have come from.

Blues scale patterns in C

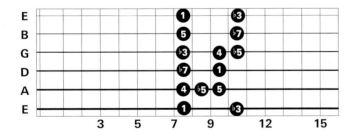

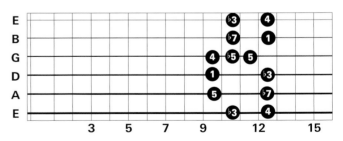

This blues solo (Exercise 121) uses the whole range of expressive techniques, including bends, unison bends, slides, hammer-ons, pull-offs, and double-stops. Use the pause button on your CD player to stop the music after each phrase and then try to echo what you have just heard. Notice the call and response structure of the phrasing and remember that it is always best to learn music in phrases.

the electric guitar handbook

EXERCISE 121, CD TRACK 87 / Blues in C solo

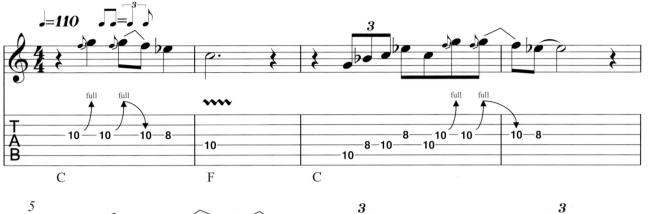

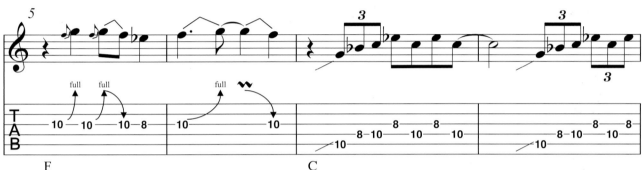

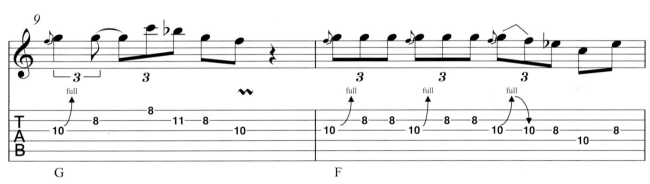

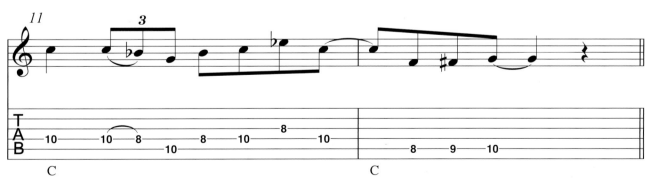

continued over page

the electric guitar handbook

EXERCISE 121 *continued*

The first chorus begins with a bend followed by a bend-and-release; watch out for the vibrato at the end of this phrase in bar two. As well as the legato and fluid style of the solo as a whole, here are some more points to watch out for. Bar six has a slow bend to which vibrato is added, followed by a slow release. Bar ten begins with some unison bends in Chuck Berry style.

The second chorus features the 'breaks' mentioned earlier, which end with the very effective double-stops in bar 16. Use finger one at the eighth fret and finger three at the tenth fret in bars 17 and 18. In bars 21 and 22 we have the climax of the solo using the highest notes from blues scale shape two. Remember the higher you go, the more exciting the music, so save the highest notes for the most intense moments of your own solos.

There are many advanced techniques in this solo and you should be prepared to spend some time mastering all of them. Then record yourself playing your own backing track and use the techniques you've learned to make up your own solo. Go ahead – steal these ideas! Mess around with them and make them your own.

Staying with the blues and blues scales, Exercise 122 is a jazz-inspired piece. There is no need for any rhythm guitar part, as we have both lead and rhythm on one guitar, which means alternating between playing chords and playing single notes. First we have a four-bar intro, based on the blues scale and using the hammer-on lick that we first saw in Exercise 87. Back then it was in the key of G, at the third fret, but now we are in the key of C at the eighth fret.

Chords for Exercise 122

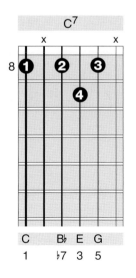

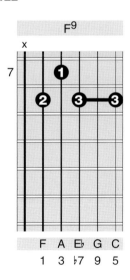

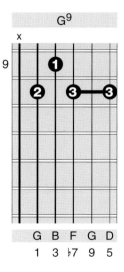

The main part of the piece is a 12-bar blues which, like Exercises 119 and 121, goes to chord IV (F9) in the second bar. We are once again using call and response, or question and answer, and the question takes the form of chords with a one-fret chromatic slide. These are then answered by the blues scale lick from the intro. Notice that the lick uses just a tiny fragment of the blues scale – more notes do not necessarily make for better music.

PRO TIP
Jazzy tones are more likely to be found using the front or neck pickup on your guitar. The amp is set clean and mellow without too much treble. This example was played on a Strat, which proves that you don't have to go out and buy one of those big hollow-body jazz guitars just yet!

■ THEORY
We have seen that chords are built using the root, third, fifth, seventh, and in the case of the F9 chord, ninth as well. Notice that if we add the ninth to a major triad the chord is an added ninth (add9), but if the seventh is present as well, it's called a ninth chord. Take a look at these chord spellings, which should make this clearer:

F = F A C
F7 = F A C E♭
Fmaj7 = F A C E
Fadd9 = F A C G
F9 = F A C E♭ G
Fmaj9= F A C E G

EXERCISE 122, CD TRACK 88 / 'Jazzy Blues'

the electric guitar handbook

PUTTING IT ALL TOGETHER

EXERCISE 123, **CD TRACK 89** / 'Brown Study'

Exercise 123, 'Brown Study,' is based on just two two-bar grooves. As with any groove-based music there is a good deal of repetition – notice the repeat signs and the 'X4' signs at the end of each two-bar section; this means play each section four times altogether.

Playing a repetitive groove is one of the hardest things to get right and requires a great deal of relaxed mental focus. You may find your concentration wandering and small timing errors creeping in. If your attention wanders, just bring your focus to the backing track, aiming to fit in with the other instruments. Sit out for the first four bars while the bass and drums set up the groove.

The notes of the guitar part are based almost entirely upon the underlying chords of A7 and D9. Begin with a one-fret slide on the D and G strings, and play the double-stops on the top two strings with finger three at the seventh fret and finger one at the fifth fret, one finger stopping both strings. In bar seven the riff is varied with a busier rhythm and the addition of chromatic passing notes on the sixth fret. At bar nine the opening riff returns and we groove off into the sunset.

PRO TIP

Picking just two notes on the inner strings of the guitar can be tricky. It is important to be able to use the fret-hand fingers to mute unwanted strings as well as to hold down the notes you want to hear. Then you won't have to be worried about hitting unwanted notes with the pick and your strumming can be more relaxed.

■ THEORY

Musicians often refer to the feel of this style of music as 'funky 16s,' as the underlying beat is the 16th-note. Practice moving your picking hand across the guitar in time with the 16th-note rhythm, and you should find that the pick directions make sense.

EXERCISE 124, CD TRACK 90 / 'Heavy Reign'

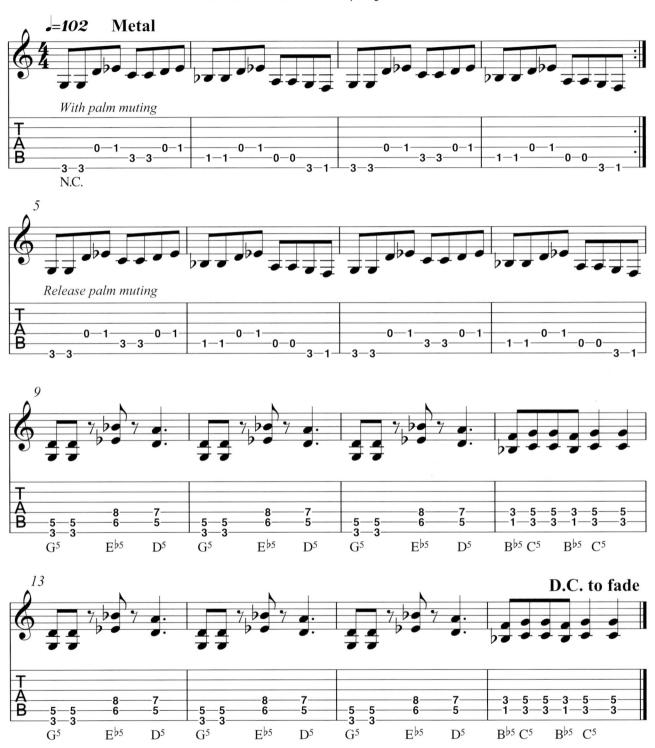

In complete contrast to the cool grooves of funk, Exercise 124 takes us into the heavy world of single-note riffing, metal-style. You may recognize the dark flavor of this music compared with some of the blues-based music we've looked at so far. Like Exercise 102 (CD track 73) the music is based on a minor scale (known as the 'natural minor' or Aeolian mode) rather than a blues scale. We are in the key of G minor.

The piece begins with a tightly muted four-bar section, which is then repeated. The same material is then played once more but without the palm muting. Have a listen and notice how the music seems to open up when you release the muting. This is helped by the opening of the high hat in the drum part. Then we are into some heavy 5 chords before the whole piece is repeated, fading towards the end on the second time through.

The guitar part was played using the bridge pickup of a Strat with a distortion pedal before the amp. In this guitar sound there are lots of mid and high frequencies and not too much bass; this helps to avoid the muddiness that distortion can sometimes cause.

■ THEORY

This piece introduces the sign D.C. at the end, which is short for 'Da Capo.' This means 'from the top,' and is musical shorthand for 'play the whole piece again from the beginning.'

Exercise 125 consists of two versions of the G minor scale. It is shown first as a shape using open strings and then as a movable shape that can be played in any key. The

PRO TIP

When you play the 5-chord shape on the fourth and fifth strings be sure to mute the sixth string of the tip of your first finger.

EXERCISE 125 / G minor scales

continued over page

the electric guitar handbook

EXERCISE 125 *continued*

open-string shape is used in the riff section of 'Heavy Reign.' Although this is the easier shape to play, it is not a movable shape, as it includes open-string notes.

Both scale shapes use all the notes from the key that can be played without changing position. Classical guitar players tend to learn scales from one root note to the next, (for example, from the root note G to the G an octave or two octaves higher). Electric guitar players are interested in playing all the notes in the key that can be reached from any one position, as this approach is more useful for making up riffs and for improvising solos.

PRO TIP

When playing seven-note scales like this you often need to stretch your hand out over five frets, as on the D-string here (movable shape). Try using fingers one, two, and four instead of the more obvious one, three, and four.

Exercise 126, 'Wireless World,' is an indie rock track inspired by bands like Radiohead and Coldplay. The track begins with four bars of solo drums, and then adds, one by one, an arpeggio guitar part, a melody-line guitar part, and finally a lead guitar solo.

Guitar one plays an arpeggiated chord sequence. If you have a close look you will notice that the top three notes of these chords are the same for the first three shapes. What is happening is that the D major chord rings on through the first six bars but the bass note changes to B after two bars and then to G two bars later. We have called the second chord B minor seven, but we could have called it D/B, in the same way that we've called the third chord D/G. Just in case you don't remember seeing this type of

EXERCISE 126, **CD TRACK 91** / 'Wireless World' guitar one

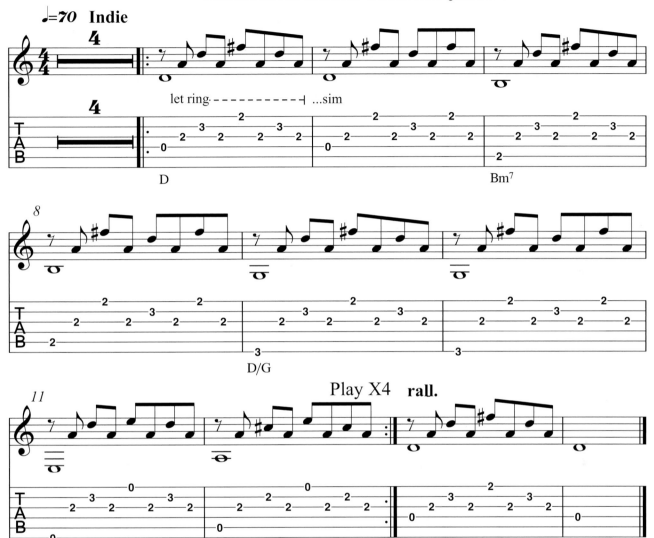

the electric guitar handbook

PUTTING IT ALL TOGETHER

Chords for 'Wireless World'

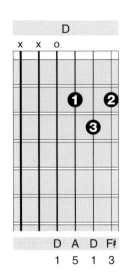

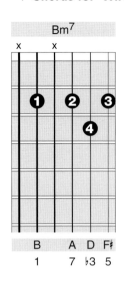

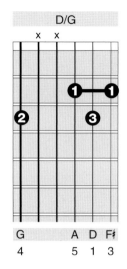

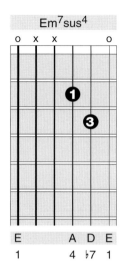

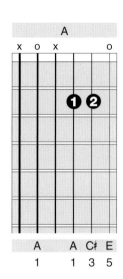

chord before, they are known as 'slash chords.' It is a way of adding the bass note of your choice to any chord.

The track was played with a pick using strict down/up alternation, but you could try it fingerstyle, using your thumb (p) to play the bass note at the beginning of the bar and then index (i) middle (m) and ring (a) fingers to play the notes on the top three strings, keeping one finger for each string. Don't forget that you have to let the notes ring on, and that the eight-bar sequence is played four times altogether. This guitar part was played on a Strat using the 'in-between' position of bridge and middle pickup together.

■ THEORY

The word 'rall…' over the last two bars is short for 'rallentando,' an Italian word meaning 'slowing down.'

After four bars of drums and eight bars of guitar one, guitar two enters with a simple melody played mostly on the D-string (Exercise 127). The part is eight bars long, made from a two-bar melody played three times (that's six bars) with new material in bars seven and eight. The first note of each two-bar phrase matches the bass note played by guitar one. This part was played on the front pickup of a Strat, and uses a fuller and more rounded tone than guitar one. Play firmly and evenly and as legato as possible.

After 20 bars guitar three enters with a characteristically quirky solo (Exercise 128). Notice that the 20-bar rest is written in sections – four bars, eight bars, eight bars, etc – which helps you to count through the empty bars. Often in written music you will also see 'drum solo,' 'guitar enters' and so on above the rest bars to help you keep track of where you are.

the electric guitar handbook

EXERCISE 127, CD TRACK 91 / 'Wireless World' guitar two

the electric guitar handbook

EXERCISE 128, CD TRACK 91 / 'Wireless World' guitar three

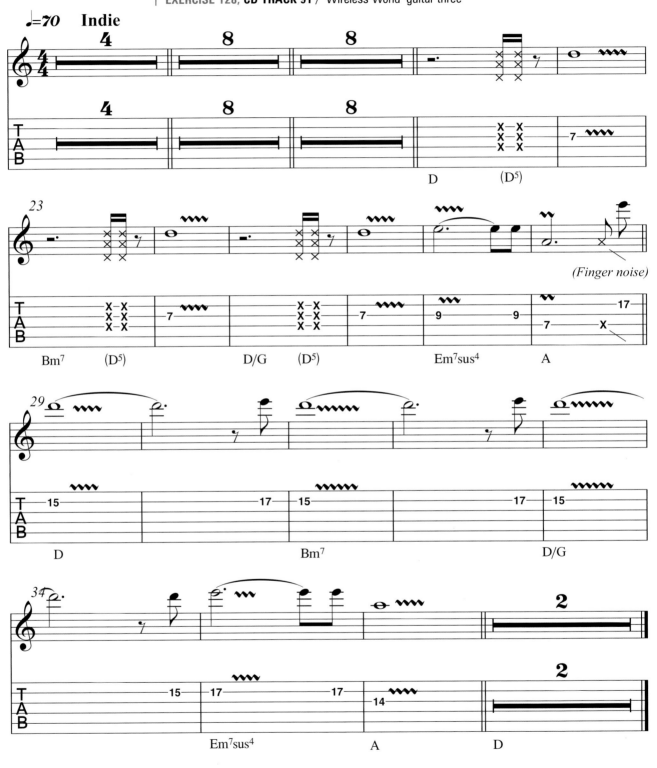

the electric guitar handbook

PUTTING IT ALL TOGETHER

We begin with a percussive, fret-hand muted D5 chord. Don't actually hold the strings down, just touch the strings lightly with your fingertips and make a quick and firm down and up stroke with the pick. You should hear the sort of percussive tone heard on the CD. Next, using finger one, play the seventh fret on the G-string and hold the note, creating a smooth vibrato by pulling and releasing the string in the direction of the B-string. Good vibrato is regular and even and is one of the expressive ways in which the guitar imitates the human voice. It also adds sustain.

This piece was played using the bridge pickup on the same Strat, plugged into a distortion box and a chorus pedal. The chorus effect is slight, but adds some interest and complexity to the long notes.

You may have heard tracks with several layers of guitar that appear to be all playing the same melody in harmony. Brian May of Queen is one artist whose playing is particularly associated with this style. In Exercise 129, guitar one is playing the lowest part of a three-part harmony, starting with a bend on the ninth fret of the G-string.

Push the string across the guitar until it rises two frets in pitch, then release it back down. Then pick the seventh fret and ninth fret and again bend up to the 11th fret. All this can be done with just fingers one and three of your fret hand, and you should keep finger one down throughout to help with the bending when using finger three. Notice the repeat signs and the instruction to play four times. The last four bars consist of a

PRO TIP

It's important to be able to bend in tune. When practicing this piece, try picking the 11th fret on the G-string before you bend the ninth fret; this way, you will train yourself to hear the target pitch before you begin

EXERCISE 129, CD TRACK 92 / Harmony guitars one

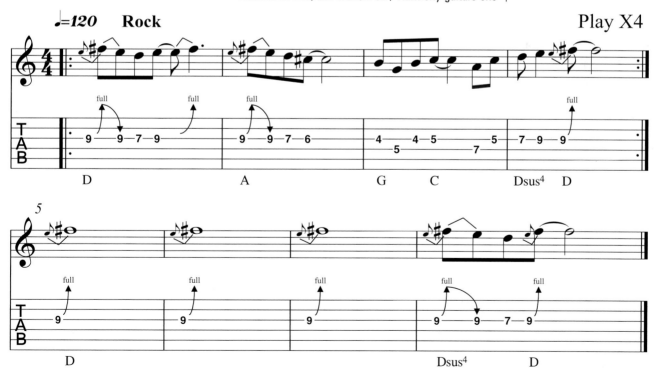

the electric guitar handbook

PRO TIP

If you can hear some music in your head, but you can't seem to find it on your instrument, try singing it first. Your voice is your inbuilt instrument and has a direct connection to your ear. If you can sing something, you will be closer to finding those same notes on the frets.

held bend, again on the ninth fret, with a bend-and-release combination in the final bar. You will need a singing tone with lots of sustain. This example was played using both distortion and chorus, on the bridge pickup of a Strat.

■ THEORY

This piece of music is in the key of D major and the piece begins on a D major chord. This chord contains three notes, D, F-sharp and A, and we begin with a bend up to F-sharp at the 11th fret. So we are starting on the third of the chord. As we will see, each of the other parts will begin on a different note of the chord.

Guitar two (Exercise 130) has the highest part for the first eight bars. It exactly parallels guitar one, except that it begins on the B-string with a bend up to the note A, the fifth of the D major chord. Start with finger two on the eighth fret of the B-string and a bend and release as before. Again, it would be best to keep finger one at the seventh fret and use it to help with bending.

Bands very rarely have three guitar players, so what should you do if you wish to add a third harmony guitar part? Well, if you're playing live, guitar one could switch to the guitar three part after eight bars. If you're in the studio, you can overdub (ie, add an extra part to what you've recorded already).

EXERCISE 130, CD TRACK 92 / Harmony guitars two

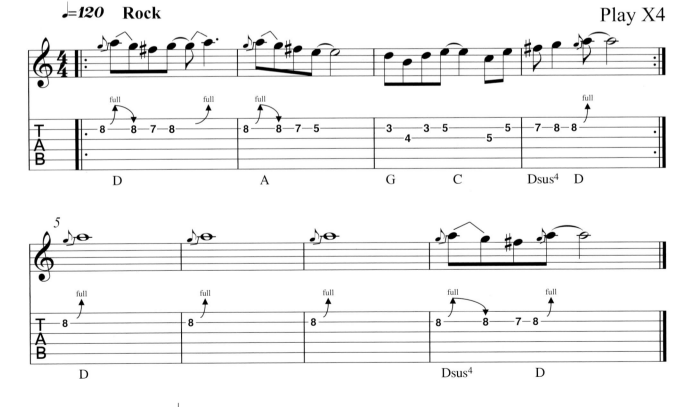

EXERCISE 131, CD TRACK 92 / Harmony guitars three

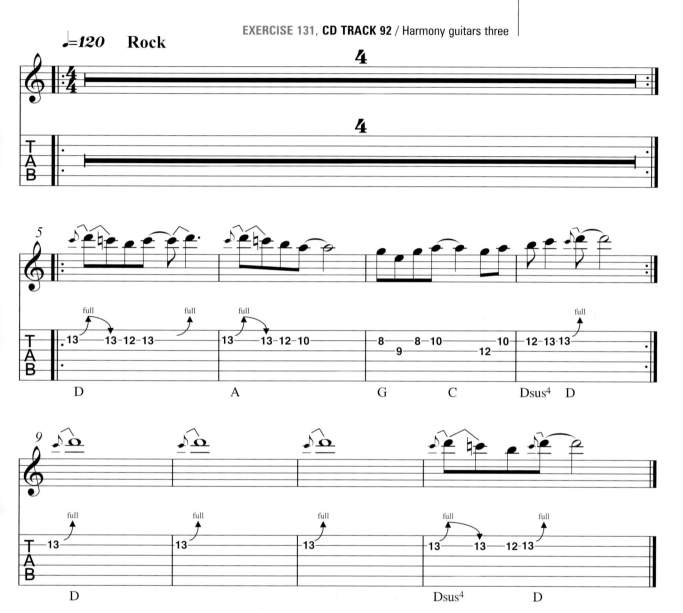

Exercise 131 is guitar three, the highest part. Entering after eight bars, it begins with a bend up to the note D, which is the root note of the D major chord. So each of the three guitar parts begins with a bend to a separate note of the chord. Sometimes the notes that fit and make good harmony parts are easy to find; at other times you may need some trial and error. One note that works just as well as the root, third, and fifth is the sixth. If you look at bars seven and eight of this example, you will see that the sixth is sounded against the G, C, and D chords (the notes E, A, and B respectively). This note may not seem an obvious choice so remember to try it if you're working out some harmony guitar parts.

the electric guitar handbook

Exercise 132, 'Mars Attacks,' is an 'indie jangle' style track that takes a selection of the added-note chords, pedal notes, triads, and arpeggios we've learned and mixes them into one seamless whole. The first eight bars are the introduction; notice that all these chords are extended or altered in some way to create the rich, chiming tones we are looking for.

At bar nine we get into some syncopated rhythmic strumming, where the lower notes of the chord change while the top notes stay the same. There is an open E and third-fret D pedal above the first three chords of the four-chord sequence. The chord shapes should be familiar from earlier exercises we have looked at, but if you don't recognize them as shapes the tab will show you which notes to hold down.

The four-chord sequence is played for a third time (bars 13-14) and at bar 15 we have a new rhythm and just one chord per bar. This is the start of a climbing four-bar phrase that uses the open E and B-strings as a pedal and leads into the main theme at bar 19. At this point you need to focus all your strumming on the highest four strings. This figure plays around with added notes, often doubling the fretted E and the open E.

The theme introduced at bar 19 continues until bar 27, at which point the music of the intro returns with a modified rhythm and some variations in the arpeggio figures.

There is some fast strumming in this track that will be tricky if you're not used to it. Remember to keep your hand moving four strokes to a beat: down-up-down-up on

PRO TIP

Remember that you don't have to hit all six strings every time when you strum. Follow the music and hit all six only on accented beats; if you write your own music in this way you will find your strumming sounds more interesting than if you just bang away at all six strings all the time.

EXERCISE 132, CD TRACK 93 / 'Mars Attacks'

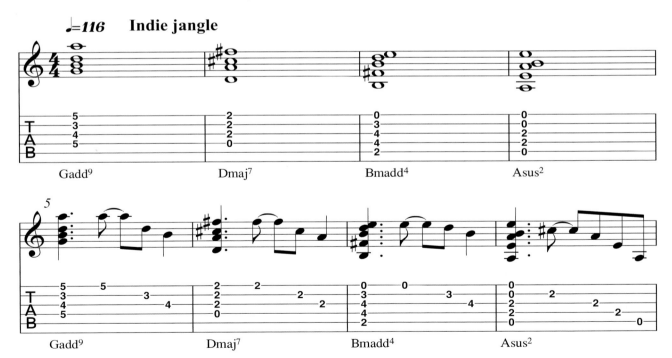

the electric guitar handbook

EXERCISE 132 *continued*

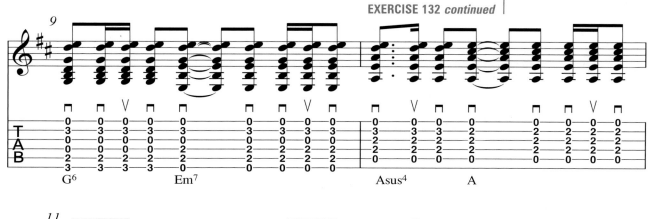

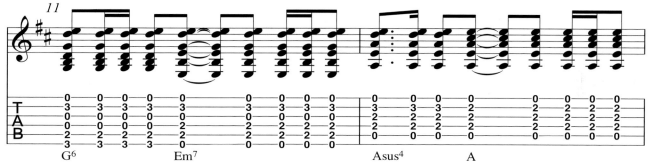

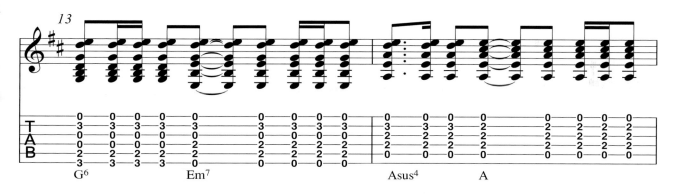

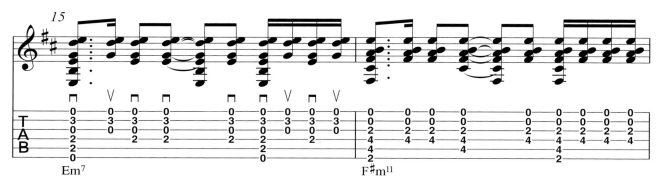

continued over page

the electric guitar handbook

EXERCISE 132 *continued*

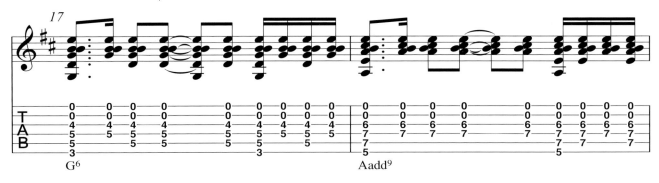

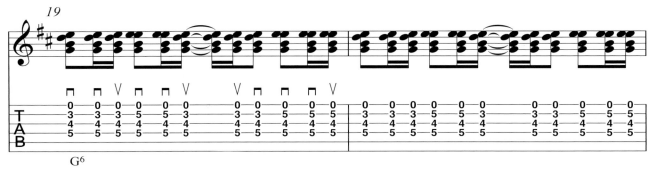

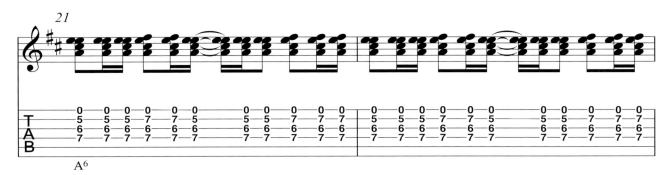

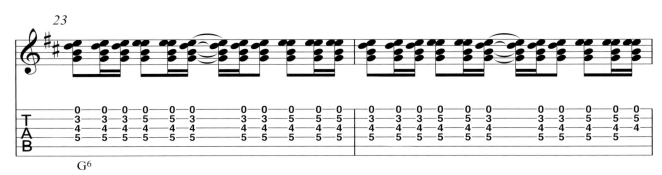

the electric guitar handbook

EXERCISE 132 *continued*

the electric guitar handbook

each beat. Play gently at first and aim to just skim the strings with the pick. If you have a metronome, try learning the strumming one bar at a time at a slower tempo, and then gradually increase the speed until your playing is as fast as the CD track.

Exercise 133 picks up where Part Three, Section Three left off, and brings together harmonics, two-hand tapping, picking with the bar and similar techniques to make a crazy off-the-wall solo.

We kick off with some triads (like those in Exercise 115) played here using the volume control of the guitar to create a fade-in or 'swell' effect. Wrap your smallest finger around the volume control and turn down, then strike the chord, and turn back up.

Then it's on to some fast single-note runs, playing six notes to a beat (sextuplets). Bars five and six of this track make use of a finger pattern using fingers one, two, and four, back and forth on adjacent strings. Most of the notes seem to come from a G major scale, though the C-sharps don't belong. The pattern carries on to the second and first strings and at this point you have D-sharps and G-sharps and the notes don't fit any particular scale. For this reason I call it a finger pattern rather than a scale; you can play all kinds of so-called 'wrong' notes if you can play fast enough!

Notice that in fast legato passages you can tap 'from nowhere' with your fret hand and it sounds like you picked the note. This legato section ends with harmonics, before moving on to a tricky left-hand pull-off pattern in bar eight.

Bar nine is similar to Exercise 113, 'picking with the bar,' except that in this example the fret-hand notes are in octaves, sliding fingers one and three up the guitar together. In bar ten we have a phrase of unison bends which lead, at bar 11, into a sequence of fast, descending three-note arpeggios played by tapping and pulling off the first of each group with the pick hand. At the end of bar 12 and all through bar 13 we have a sequence of three-note hammer-ons moving progressively across the guitar.

The second half of bar 14 brings in a new technique known as tremolo picking, which is extremely fast alternate picking (notice how this is written). We then move on to the climax of the solo, which is a fast two-hand tapping riff between the 12th, seventh, and fifth frets, nine notes to a beat, ending in an A5 chord.

This solo can be viewed as a collection of riffs, tricks and distinctive sounds, and it serves to illustrate that modern rock guitar solos don't necessarily have to be based on the blues approach of call and response. Phrasing is still important, however, and though there's a crazy randomness to all that happens here, there is still an underlying logic which seems to string the phrases together and make the piece work as a whole.

EXERCISE 133, CD TRACK 94 / Soloing showcase

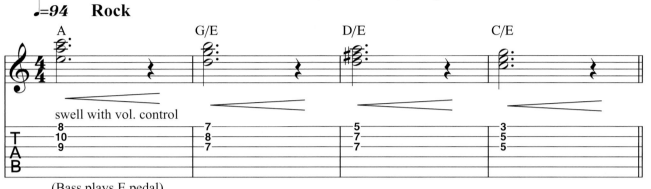

♩=94   **Rock**

swell with vol. control

(Bass plays E pedal)

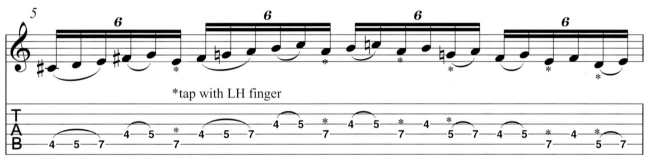

*tap with LH finger

(Bass plays A pedal from now on)

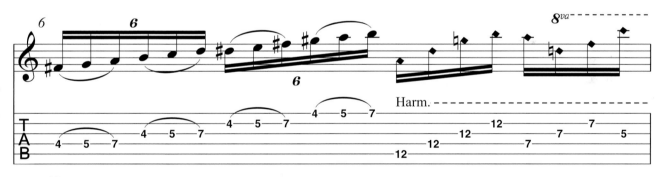

Harm.

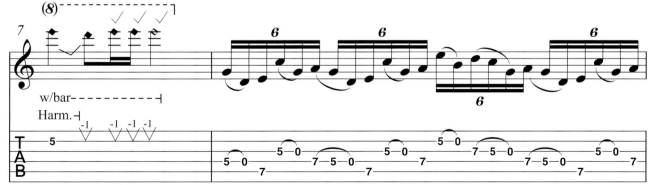

w/bar
Harm.

continued over page

the electric guitar handbook

EXERCISE 133 *continued*

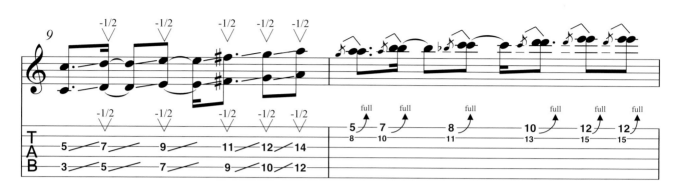

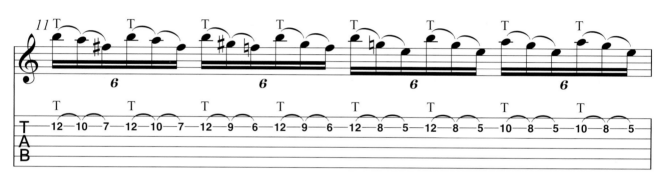

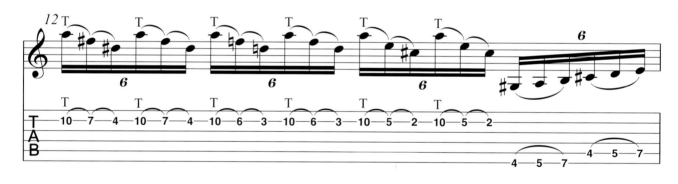

EXERCISE 133 *continued*

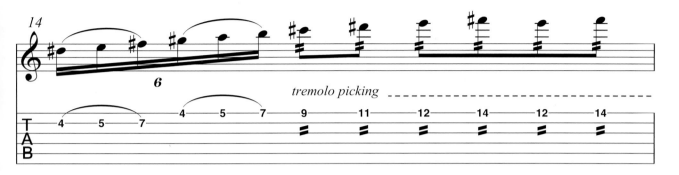

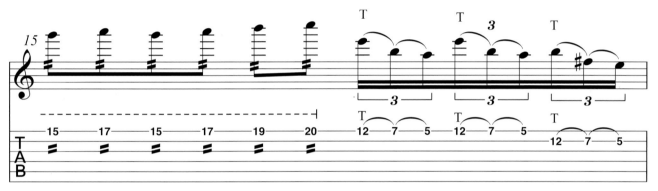

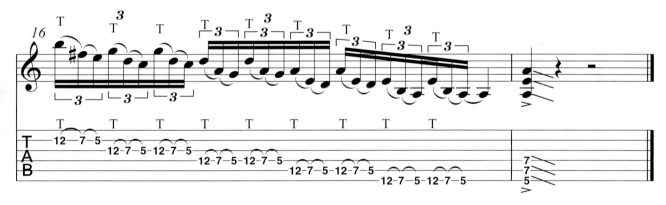

the electric guitar handbook

FURTHER STUDY

There are many books available that feature accurate transcriptions of guitar parts from CDs. Pick your favorite band/guitarist and get shopping! If you decide to specialize in a particular style you will also find study material available devoted to every possible genre – including some you've never heard of. Most of all, practice learning from the music you listen to, figuring out the chords and guitar parts from your own music collection. Try slowing the music down if it's too difficult. The internet is also a great source of tab, but remember to use your ear as it's not always all that accurate.

SUMMING UP

If you've reached this stage in the book you can be confident that your guitar playing has developed way beyond the beginner stage and you're pretty much ready for anything. I hope you've enjoyed the music and wish you the very best in your guitar playing in the future.

APPENDIX

Spellings of common chords

TYPE OF CHORD	NAME OF CHORD	SYMBOL	SPELLING
Triads:	C major	C	C E G
	C minor	Cm	C E♭ G
	C diminished	Cdim, C°	C Eb G♭
	C augmented	Caug, C+	C E G♯
Sixths	C sixth	C6	C E G A
	C minor sixth	Cm6, C-6	C E♭ G A
Sevenths	C major seven	Cmaj7, Cma7, C△7	C E G B
	C seven	C7	C E G B♭
	C minor seven	Cm7, C-7	C Eb G B♭
	C minor seven flat five	Cm7♭5,	C E♭ G♭ B♭
	C "half diminished"	Cø	
	C diminished seven	C°7, Cdim7	C E♭ G♭ A (B♭♭)
Ninths	C major nine	Cmaj9, C△9	C E G B D
	C nine	C9	C E G B♭ D
	C minor nine	Cm9, C-9	C E♭ G B♭ D
	C added ninth	Cadd9	C E G D
Elevenths	C eleven	C11	C (E G) B♭ D F
Suspended Chords	C suspended fourth	Csus4	C F G
	C suspended second	Csus2	C D G

the electric guitar handbook

Complete notes of guitar including fret positions and music notation

▪on the cd

1. Tuning tones
2. Exercise 1, open string notes
3. Exercise 2, counting beats
4. Exercise 3, 'Open Season'
5. Exercise 4, the D-string
6. Exercise 5, 'The Low Down'
7. Exercise 7, 'First String Thing'
8. Exercise 8, introducing 3/4
9. Exercise 10, 'Blues One'
10. Exercise 12, 'Blues Two'
11. Exercise 13, upstrokes and downstrokes
12. Exercise 14, 'Blues Three'
13. Exercise 16, 'Blues Four'
14. Exercise 18, one-octave chromatic scale
15. Exercise 19, 'Shadow Walk'; Exercise 62, 'Shadow Walk' rhythm part
16. Exercise 21, 'Swamp Thing'
17. Exercise 23, 'Defective Detective'
18. Exercise 25, 'E-string Boogie'
19. Exercise 26, 'Rock'n'roll in A'
20. Exercise 28, 'Movable Metal'; Exercise 77, 'Movable Metal' rhythm part
21. Exercise 29, 'John Lee'
22. Exercise 30, blues scale in E
23. Exercise 31, 'Double-stop Blues'; Exercise 43, 12-bar blues in E
24. Exercise 32, 'Midnight Metal'
25. Exercise 33, minor pentatonic scale in E
26. Exercise 34, C and G major pentatonic scales
27. Exercise 35, 'Country Cousin'
28. Exercise 36, 'Finger-Licking Good'
29. Exercise 37, C major scale
30. Exercise 39, blues vamp on A
31. Exercise 40, vamp with palm muting
32. Exercise 41, blues vamp on E

33. Exercise 42, 12-bar blues in A
34. Exercise 44, 12-bar shuffle in A
35. Exercise 45, E blues rhythm, solo one, solo two
36. Exercise 49, E major chord
37. Exercise 50, more chords
38. Exercise 51, majors moving
39. Exercise 52, 'Joe Strumming'
40. Exercise 53, 'Slight Return'
41. Exercise 54, 'Minor Mishap'
42. Exercise 55, 'Big Chords One'
43. Exercise 56, 'Low Strum, High Strum'
44. Exercise 57, 'Low Strum, High Strum' with bassline
45. Exercise 58, 'Big Chords Two'
46. Exercise 59, G and C root and fifth
47. Exercise 60, 'Twang Thang'
48. Exercise 61, 'Drive-in Groove'
49. Exercise 63, 'Big Chords One' lead part
50. Exercise 64, 'Big Chords Two' lead part
51. Exercise 65, 'Buck The Trend'
52. Exercise 66, 'Faithless'
53. Exercise 67, 'Stay The Same'; Exercise 71, 'Stay The Same' rhythm part
54. Exercise 68, rock arpeggios
55. Exercise 69, rock arpeggios two
56. Exercise 72, 'Fives And Nines' rhythm part
57. Exercise 73, extended chord shapes
58. Exercise 74, bar chords and added notes
59. Exercise 76, 'Positive Pedal'
60. Exercise 78, 'Drop D'
61. Exercise 79, A5 plus riff
62. Exercise 80, grunge-style riffs
63. Exercise 81, 'Steady As A Rock' vamp; Exercise 96, 'Steady As A Rock' lead part
64. Exercise 82, 'Chili California'; Exercise 83, 'Chili California' lead part

65. Exercise 84, two-octave blues scale in A
66. Exercise 85, blues riffs
67. Exercises 87-88, 'Funky Junction'
68. Exercise 89, bends, vibrato, and triplet runs
69. Exercise 91, 'Jimmy Or Jimi?'; Exercise 92, 'Jimmy Or Jimi?' rhythm part
70. Exercise 93, rock'n'roll Chuck-style
71. Exercise 94, 'Joe Meets Eddie'
72. Exercise 99, 'Twang Thang' lead part
73. Exercise 102, F-sharp minor metal riffs
74. Exercise 105, metal riffs in E minor
75. Exercise 106, 'Fives And Nines' lead part
76. Exercise 107, natural harmonics
77. Exercise 108, artificial and tapped harmonics
78. Exercise 109, two-hand tapping
79. Exercise 111, chordal tapping
80. Exercise 112, Van Halen tapping
81. Exercise 113, whammy bar tricks
82. Exercise 114, arpeggios and bar chords with pedals
83. Exercise 115, triads with pedal notes
84. Exercise 116, triads, sus4 chords, and E pedal
85. Exercise 117, 'Dr Punkenstein'
86. Exercise 118, Motown-style rhythm part
87. Exercise 119, blues in C rhythm part; Exercise 121, blues in C solo
88. Exercise 122, 'Jazzy Blues';
89. Exercise 123, 'Brown Study'
90. Exercise 124, 'Heavy Reign'
91. Exercises 126-128, 'Wireless World'
92. Exercises 129-131, harmony guitars
93. Exercise 132, 'Mars Attacks'
94. Exercise 133, soloing showcase